RED-ROBIN

JANE ABBOTT

1st WORLD
LIBRARY
Literary Society

Red-Robin

Jane Abbott

© 1st World Library, 2006
PO Box 2211
Fairfield, IA 52556
www.1stworldlibrary.com
First Edition

LCCN: 2006935239

Softcover ISBN: 1-4218-2492-2
Hardcover ISBN: 1-4218-2392-6
eBook ISBN: 1-4218-2592-9

Purchase *"Red-Robin"*
as a traditional bound book at:
www.1stWorldLibrary.com/purchase.asp?ISBN=1-4218-2492-2

1st World Library is a literary, educational organization
dedicated to:

- Creating a free internet library of downloadable ebooks

- Hosting writing competitions and offering book
publishing scholarships.

Interested in more 1st World Library books?
contact: literacy@1stworldlibrary.com
Check us out at: www.1stworldlibrary.com

1ˢᵗ World Library Literary Society

Giving Back to the World

"If you want to work on the core problem, it's early school literacy."

- James Barksdale, former CEO of Netscape

"No skill is more crucial to the future of a child, or to a democratic and prosperous society, than literacy."

- Los Angeles Times

Literacy... means far more than learning how to read and write... The aim is to transmit... knowledge and promote social participation."

- UNESCO

"Literacy is not a luxury, it is a right and a responsibility. If our world is to meet the challenges of the twenty-first century we must harness the energy and creativity of all our citizens."

- President Bill Clinton

"Parents should be encouraged to read to their children, and teachers should be equipped with all available techniques for teaching literacy, so the varying needs and capacities of individual kids can be taken into account."

- Hugh Mackay

TO BETSY

CONTENTS

PROLOGUE

A STORY BEFORE THE STORY

On a green hillside a girl lay prone in the sweet grass, very still that she might not, by the slightest quiver, disturb the beauty that was about her. There was so very, very *much* beauty - the sky, azure blue overhead and paling where it touched the green-fringed earth; the whispering tree under which she lay, the lush meadow grass, moving like waves of a sea, the bird nesting above her, everything -

And Moira O'Donnell, who had never been farther than the boundaries of her county, knew the whole world was beautiful, too.

Behind her, hid in a hollow, stood the small cottage where, at that very moment, her grandmother was preparing the evening meal. And, beyond, in the village was the little old stone church and Father Murphy's square bit of a house with its wide doorstep and its roof of thatch, and Widow Mulligan's and the Denny's and the Finnegan's and all the others.

Moira loved them all and loved the hospitable homes where there was always, in spite of poverty, a bounty of good feeling.

And before her, just beyond that last steep rise, was the sea. She could hear its roar now, like a deep voice drowning the clearer pipe of the winging birds and the shrill of the little grass creatures. Often she went down to its edge, but at this hour she liked best to lie in the grass and dream her dreams to its lifting music.

Her dream always began with: "Oh, Moira O'Donnell, it's all yours! It's all yours!" Which, of course, sounded like boasting, or a miser gloating over his gold, and might have seemed very funny to anyone so stupid as to see only the girl's shabby dress and her bare feet, gleaming like white satin against the green of the grass. But no fine lady in that land felt richer than Moira when she began her dreaming.

Of late, her dreams were taking on new shapes, as though, with her growth, they reached out, too. And today, as she lay very still in the grass, something big, that was within her and yet had no substance, lifted and sung up to the blue arch of the sky and on to the sun and away westward with it, away like a bird in far flight.

Beyond that golden horizon of heaving sea was everything one could possibly want; Moira had heard that when she was a tiny girl. America, the States, they were words that opened fairy doors.

Father Murphy had told her much about that world beyond the sea. He had visited it once; had spent six weeks with his sister who had married and settled on a farm in the state of Ohio. His sister's husband had all sorts of new-fangled machinery for plowing and seeding, and for his reaping! And Father Murphy had told her of the free library that was in the town near his sister's home, where he could sit all day and read to his heart's content.

Father Murphy (he had spent three whole days in New York) had made her see the great buildings that were like granite giants towering over and walling in the pigmy humanity that beat against their sides like the rise and fall of the tide; he told her of the rush and roar of the streets and of the trains that tore over one's head.

Jane Abbott

And he told her of the loveliness that was there in picture and music. Moira, listening, quivering with the longing to be fine and to do fine things, could always see it all just as though magic hands swept aside those miles of ocean dividing that land of marvel from her Ireland.

That was why it was so simple to let her dream-mind climb up and away westward. Her eyes, staring into the paling blue, saw beautiful things and her thoughts revelled in delicious fancies.

That slender, gold crowned bit of a cloud - *that* was Destiny circling her globe, weaving, and moulding, and shaping; Moira O'Donnell's own humble thread was on her loom! And Destiny's face was turned westward. Moira saw shining towers and thronged streets and fields greener than her own. Far-off music sounded in her ears as though the world off there just sang with gladness. And it was waiting for her - her. She saw herself moving forward to it all with quick step and head high, going to a beautiful goal. Sometimes that goal was a palace-place, encircled by brilliant flowers, sometimes a farm like Father Murphy's sister's and a husband who worked with marvelous contrivances, sometimes a free library with all the books one could want, sometimes a dim, vaulted space through which echoed exquisite music -

She so loved that make-believe Moira, moving forward toward glowing things, that she cried aloud: "That's me! *Me*!" And of course her voice broke the spell - the dream vanished; there was nothing left but the fleecy cloud, the meadow lark's song, close by.

There was just time enough before her grandmother needed her, to run down to Father Murphy's. She knew at this hour she would find him by his wide doorstep. Fleetly, her bare feet scarcely touching the soft earth, she covered the distance to his house. She ran up behind him and slipped her fingers over his half-closed eyes.

He knew the familiar touch of the girl's hands. He patted

them with his own and moved aside on his bench that she might sit down with him.

"Father," she said, very low, her eyes shining. "It's my dream again."

The old priest did not chide her for idling, as her grandmother would have done. The old priest dreamed, too.

"Tell me," she went on. "Can one go to school over there as long as one likes? Is it too grown-up I am to learn more things from books?"

The old Father told her one could never be too old to learn from books. He loved her craving for knowledge. Had he not taught her himself, since she was twelve? He looked at her proudly.

"Father!" She whispered now, and the rose flush deepened in her face. "It's Danny Lynch that comes every evening to see me."

Now Father Murphy turned squarely and regarded her with startled eyes. This slip of a girl was the most precious colleen in his flock.

"And, Father, it's of America *he* talks all the time!"

The old priest shivered as though from a chill. Sensing his feeling, Moira caught his hand quickly and held it in a close grip.

"But if I go away it's not forgetting you I'll be! Oh, who in all this world has been a better friend to Moira O'Donnell? Who has taught Moira but you?"

"Child -"

"Sure it's grown-up I am! See!" She sprang to her feet and

stood slimly erect. "See?"

He nodded slowly. "Yes. And your old priest had not noticed. Moira -" he caught her arm, leaned forward and peered into her face as though to see through it into her soul. "Moira, girl, is it courage I have taught ye? And honor? And faith?"

Her heart was singing now over the secret she had shared with him. Who would not have courage and faith when one was so happy? With a lift of her shoulders, a tilt of her head, she shrugged away his seriousness.

"If you could only see me, Father, as I am in my dream. Oh, it's beautiful I am! And smart! And rich!"

"Not money," broke in the priest with a ring of contempt.

"Sure, no, not money! But fine things. Oh, Father," she clasped her hands childishly. "It's fine things I want. The very finest in the world! And I want my Danny to want them, too."

"Fine things," he repeated slowly. "And will ye know the fine things from the dross, child? That wealth is more times what ye give, aye, than what ye get? It's rich ye are of your fine things if the heart of you is unselfish -"

"What talk, you, Father; it's like the croaking frogs in the Widow Finnegan's pond you are! But, sh-h-h, I will tell you what I saw, real as real, as I lay dreaming - Destiny herself, as fine as you please, sailing to the new world, a-spinning on her loom. She had Moira O'Donnell's poor thread and who knows, Father Murphy, but maybe this minute it's a-spinning it with a thread of gold she is!" The girl's eyes danced. "Ah, 'tis nonsense I talk, for it's a dream it was, but my poor heart's so light it hurts - here."

The old man laid a trembling hand upon her head. Under his touch it bowed with quick reverence but not before she had seen a mistiness in the kindly eyes.

"It's God's blessing I ask for ye - and yes, may your dream come true -"

"Your blessing for Danny, too," whispered Moira.

"For the both of ye!"

"Sure it's a crossing Granny'll be a-giving me and no blessing," laughed the girl. It was her own word for Granny's sharp tongue. "I'd best be off, Father dear."

"Wait." The old man disappeared through his door. Presently he came out carrying a small box. From this he took a crumpled package. Unwrapping the tissue folds he revealed, in the cup of his hand, a string of green beads.

"Oh! Oh! How beautiful!" cried the girl. "Are they for me?" with the youthful certainty that all lovely things were her due.

"Yes. To remember my blessing." He regarded them fondly, lifted them that she might see their beauty against the sun's glow. "'Twas in a little shop in London I found the pretty things."

Moira knew how much he must love them as a keepsake - that visit to London was only next in his heart to the trip to America. She caught his hands, beads, tissue wrappings and all.

"Oh, it's precious they are! And you too!"

The Father fastened them over the girl's shabby dress. "They are only beads," he admonished. "But it's of this day they'll remind you."

He watched Moira as she ran off down the lane. He noted the quick, sure tread of her feet, the challenging poise of her head. "Colleen -" he whispered with a smile. "Little colleen." He turned to his door and his lips, even though they still twisted

Jane Abbott

in a smile, moved as though in prayer.

"And may God keep pure the dream in the heart of ye!"

CHAPTER I

THE ORPHAN DOLL

November - and a chill wind scurrying, snapping, biting, driving before it fantastic scraps of paper, crackly leaves, a hail of fine cinders. An early twilight, gray like a mist, enveloped the city in gloom. Through it lights gleamed bravely from the grimy windows rising higher and higher to the low-hanging clouds, each thin shaft beckoning and telling of shelter and a warmth that was home.

High over the heads of the hurrying humanity in a street of tenements Moira Lynch lighted her lamp and set it close to the bare window. With her it was a ceremony. She sang as she performed the little act. Without were the shadows of the approaching night - gloom, storm, disaster, perhaps even the evil fairies; her lamp would scatter them all with its glow, just as her song drove the worries from her heart.

Her lamp lighted, she paused for a moment, her head forward, listening. Then at the sound of a light step she sprang to the door and threw it open. A wee slip of a girl, almost one with the shadows of the dingy hallway, ran into her arms.

"And it's so late you are, dearie! And so dark it's grown - and cold. Your poor little hands are blue. Why, what have you here, hidin' under your shawl? Beryl Lynch! Dear love us - a doll!" With a laugh that was like a tinkling of low pitched bells the little mother drew the treasure from its hiding place. But as

Jane Abbott

her eyes swept the silken splendor of the raiment her merriment changed to wonder and then to fear.

"You didn't - you didn't - oh, Beryl Lynch, you -"

"Steal it? No. Give me it. I - found it."

But the terror still darkened the mother's eyes.

"And where did you find it?"

"On the bench. She left it. She forgot it. Ain't it mine now?" pleadingly. "I waited, honest, but she didn't come back."

Mrs. Lynch was examining the small wonder with timid fingers, lifting fold after fold of shining satin and dainty muslin.

"Who was she?" she asked.

"A kid." Little Beryl kindled to the interest of her story. Had not something very thrilling happened in her simple life - a life the greatest interest of which was to carry to the store each day the small bundle of crocheted lace which her mother made. "She was a swell kid. She played in the park, waitin' for a big man."

"Did she talk to you?" breathlessly.

Beryl avoided this question. The beautiful little girl had *not* spoken to her, though she had hung by very close, inviting an approach with hungry eyes.

"She was just a little kid," loftily. Then, "Ain't the doll mine?"

Mrs. Lynch patted down the outermost garment. "Yes, it's yours it is, darlin'. At least -" she hesitated over a fleeting sense of justice, "maybe the little stranger will be a-coming back for her doll. It's a fair bit of dolly and it's lonesome and weeping the little mother may be this very minute -"

Beryl reached out eager arms.

"It's an orphan doll. I'll love it *hard*. Give me it. Oh," with a breath that was like a whistle. "*Ain't* she lovely? Mom, is she *too* lovely for us?"

The timid question brought a quick change in the mother's face, a kindling of a fire within the mother breast. She straightened her slender body.

"And if there's anything too good for my girlie I'd like to see it! Isn't this the land where all men are equal and my girl and boy shall have a school as good as the best and grow up to be maybe the President himself?" She repeated the words softly as though they made a creed, learned carefully and with supreme faith. Why had she come, indeed, to this crowded, noisy city from her fair home meadows if not for this promise it held out to her?

"And isn't your brother the head of his class?" she finished triumphantly. "And it's smarter than ever you'll be yourself with your little books. Oh, childy!" She caught the little girl, doll and all, into an impulsive embrace.

From it Beryl wriggled to a practical curiosity as to supper. She sniffed. Her mother nodded.

"Stew! And with *dumplin's* -" She made it sound like fairy food. "Ready to the beating when your father comes."

"Where's Dale? And Pop?"

"It's Dale's night at the store. And Pop'll be comin' along any minute. I've set the lamp for him."

"I'm hungry," Beryl complained. She sat down cross-legged on the spotless scrap of carpeting and proceeded with infinite tenderness to disrobe the doll.

"Do you think she will like it here?" she asked suddenly, looking about the humble room which for the Lynch's, served as parlor, dining-room and kitchen. Now its bareness lay wrapped in a kindly shadow through which glinted diamond sparks from much-scrubbed tin. "It's *nice -*" Beryl meditated. She loved this hour, she loved the singing tea-kettle and the smell of strong soap and her mother's face in the lamplight, with all the loud noises of the street hushed, and the ugliness outside hidden by the closed door, against the paintless boards of which had been nailed a flaming poster inviting the nation's youth to join the Navy.

"But maybe this home'll be - too different," she finished.

The mother's eyes grew moist with a quick tenderness. Her Beryl, with this wonder of a dolly in her arms! Her mind flashed over the last Christmas and the one before that when Beryl had asked Santa Claus for a "real doll" and had cried on Christmas morning because the cheap little bit of dolldom which the mother had bought out of her meagre savings would not open or shut its eyes. And now - the impudent heart of the blessed child worrying that the home wasn't good enough for the likes of the doll!

"It's a good home for her where it's loving you are to her. It's the heart and not the gold that counts. And who knows - maybe it's a bit of luck the dolly'll be a-bringing."

As though a word of familiar portent had been uttered Beryl lifted a face upon which was reflected the glow of the little mother's. Babe as she was, she knew something of the mother's faith in the fickle god of chance, a faith that helped the little woman over the rough places, that never failed to brighten her deepest gloom. Did she not staunchly believe that someday by a turn of good fortune she and her Danny would know the America and the good things of which they had dreamed, sitting in the gloaming of their Ireland, their lover's hands close clasped? But for that hope why would they have left their dear hillsides with the homely life and the kindly neighbors and good Father Murphy who had taught her from his own dog-eared books because she was eager and quick to learn? Through the fourteen years since they had come to America those girl-and-boy dreams had gone sadly astray, but the little wife still clung to the faith that they'd have the good things sometime, her Danny would get a better job and if he didn't there was young Dale, always at the head of his class in school and even the baby Beryl, as quick as anything to pick out words from her little books.

"A good luck dolly!" Beryl held the doll close. Her eyes grew round and excited. "Then I can ride all day on a 'bus and go to the Zoo, can't I? And can I have a new coat with fur? And go to Coney? And shoot the shoots? And can Dale ride a horse? And can Dale and me go across the river where it's like - that?" nodding to the poster.

Mrs. Lynch rocked furiously in her joy at Beryl's anticipations. The floor creaked and the kettle sang louder than before.

"That you can. And it'll be a fine strong, brave girl you'll be, going to school and learning more than even poor old Father Murphy knew, God love him. And by and by -"

But a heavy toiling of steps up the stairs checked her words. That slow tread was not her big Danny nor the young Dale! At a knock she flew to the door.

"Oh, and if it isn't Mister Torrence." She caught the old man who stood on the threshold and laughingly pulled him into the room. "It was afraid I was that it was bad news! Danny Lynch isn't home yet but you shall stay and eat dumplin's with us - the best outside of our Ireland -"

"No! No!" protested the old man, regretfully. "My old woman's waitin'! *Bad* news! It's *good* news I bring. Dan's had a raise. He's foreman of the gang now. And I stepped 'round to tell ye the good news and that Dan'll be a-workin' tonight with an extry shift and'll not be comin' home to dinner, worse luck for him!" sniffing appreciatively at the pleasant odor from the stove.

"A raise? My Dan a foreman?" Moira Lynch caught her hands together. "It's the good luck! And it's deservin' of it he is for no man on the docks works harder than my big Dan." Her eyes shone like two stars.

"Well, ye'll want to be a-eatin' the dumplin's so I'll go along. Good-night, Mrs. Lynch."

"God love you, Mister Torrence," whispered Moira, too overcome to manage her voice.

Closing the door behind her unexpected visitor she turned and caught the wondering Beryl into her arms.

"And I was a-thinking it would never come! It's ashamed I should be to have doubted. My big Dan!"

"Is it the dolly that's brought us the good-luck, Mom?" interrupted Beryl, round-eyed.

"A foreman!" cried the mother in the very tone she would have used if she had said "a king." She-danced about until the floor creaked threateningly. "Our good fortune is coming, my precious. And it's fine and beautiful my girl shall be with a dress as good as the next one. Wait! Wait!" She flew into the tiny bedroom, returning in a moment with a small box in her hands. From it she lifted a string of round green beads and held them laughingly before Beryl's staring eyes.

"My beads! You shall wear them this night. It's the good old Father's blessing." She clasped them about Beryl's neck, fingering them tenderly.

"Pretty beads. Pretty beads," cried the little girl.

Suddenly quieted by a rush of memories Mrs. Lynch sat down and took Beryl upon her lap. "Beryl darlin', was the likes of that other little girl - the one who forgot the dolly - fine and beautiful?"

"Oh, yes!" The child's voice carried a note of wonder.

"And you shall be fine and beautiful, too, Moira Lynch's own girl, just as I used to dream for my own self, the selfish likes o' me. You shall go to school and learn from good books. Didn't the old Father tell me of the fine schools he had seen when he visited his sister in America? And anybody can go - anybody!"

Little Beryl felt that it was a solemn moment. She lifted serious eyes. "I promise," she drawled, with a gravity out of all proportion to her six years, "I promise to go to school and learn lots like Dale and be fine and boo'ful so's my 'dopted dolly will like me as well as - that other kid. I've gotta be good 'nough for her. So there."

The child could not comprehend the obstacles which might threaten such a standard; she stared bravely into the unblinking eyes of the doll who smiled back her graven smile.

Then: "I'm hungry," she declared, suddenly deciding that dumplings were more important than anything else. "And can my Dolly sit in Pop's seat?"

"That she can," cried the mother, going to her "mixin'." "And what a gay supper it will be - with the new dolly and the pretty beads and the dumplin's. Oh, Himself a foreman!"

CHAPTER II

A PRINCE

Promptly at nine o'clock, young Dale Lynch turned the key in the door of "Tony Sebastino, Groceries" and started, whistling, homeward. Three times a week, from the close of school until nine o'clock, he worked in the store, snatching a dinner of bananas, or bread and cheese, between customers. Because "Mom" had whispered that there were to be "dumplin's" this night and that she would keep some warm for him, and because the wind whipped chillingly through his thin clothing, he broke into a run.

His homeward way led him past a bit of open triangle which in the neighborhood was dignified by the name of park, a dreary place now, dirty straw stacked about the fountain, dry leaves and papers cluttering the brown earth and whipping against the iron palings of the fence. Dale, still whistling, turned its corner and ran, full-tilt, upon a bit of humanity clinging, like the paper and leaves, to the fence.

"Giminy Gee!" Dale jumped back in alarm. Then: "Did I scare you, kid? Oh, say, what's the matter?" For the face that turned to his was red and swollen with weeping. "Y'lost?" This was Dale's natural conclusion, for the hour was late, and the child a very small one.

"I lost - my Cynthia."

"Your - *what?*"

"My - my Cynthia. She's my b-bestest doll. I forgot her." The voice trailed off in a wail.

Dale, touched by her woe, looked about him. Certainly no Cynthia was visible. By rapid questioning on his part he drew from her the story of her desertion. She had played a nice game of running 'round and 'round and counting the "things," waiting for Mr. Tony; Cynthia did not like to run because it shook her eyes, so she had put her down on the edge of the straw where the wind would not blow on her. And then Mr. Tony had come and had told her to "hustle along" and she "had runned away and for-g-got Cynthia!"

"Well, I guess she's somebody else's Cynthia now, kid. Things don't stay long in the parks 'round here."

Dale seemed so very old and very wise that the tiny girl listened to his verdict with blanching face. He knew, of course.

"Where d'you live?" demanded Dale. "Why, you're just a baby! Anybody with you?"

The child pointed rather uncertainly to one of the intersecting streets.

"I come that way," she said, then, even while saying it, began to wonder if that were the way she had come. The streets all looked so much alike. She had run along the curb, so as to be as far away as possible from the dark alley ways and the doors. And it had been a long way.

Her lip quivered though she would not cry. After Cynthia's fate, just to be lost herself did not matter.

"Well, don't you know where you live? What's the street? I'll take you home."

"22 Patchin Place," lisped the child.

Dale hesitated a moment to make sure of his bearings. "Well, then, come along. I know where that is. And you forget 'bout your Cynthia. You've got another doll, haven't you? If you haven't, you just ask Santa Claus for one. Why, say, kiddo, what's this? You lame?" For the little girl skipped jerkily at his side.

"That's just the way I'm made," the child answered, quite indifferent to the shocked note in the boy's voice. "I can walk and run, but I go crooked."

"What's your name?"

"Robin Forsyth." She made it sound like "Wobbin Force."

"Oh, Wobbin Force. Funny name, isn't it? And what's your Ma and Pa going to say to you for running off?"

Putting a small hand trustingly into the boy's big one, the child skipped along at his side. "Oh, nothing," she answered, lost in an admiring contemplation of her rescuer. "What's they, anyway?"

"A Ma? Don't you know what your mother is?"

Little Robin met his astonishment with a ripple of laughter. "Oh a *mother*! I had a lovely, lovely mother once but she's gone away - to Heaven. And is a Pa a Jimmie?"

"A - what?" Dale had never met such a strange child.

"'Cause Jimmie's my Parent. I call him Parent sometimes and sometimes I call him Jimmie."

If his companion had not been so very small Dale might have suspected an attempt at "kidding." He glanced sidewise and suspiciously at her but all he saw was a cherub face framed in a tilted sky-blue tam-o'shanter and straggling ends of flaming red hair.

"Jimmie won't scold me. *He'd* want me to try to find Cynthia." Robin smothered a sigh. "He wasn't home anyway."

"D'you live all alone? You and your Jimmie?"

"Oh, yes, only Aunt Milly's downstairs and Grandpa Jones is 'cross the hall, so I'm never 'fraid. They're not my really truly aunt's and grandfather's - I just call them that. And Jimmie leaves the light burning anyway. What's your name? And are you very old? Are you a man like Jimmie?"

Dale, warming under the adoration he saw on the small face, felt very big and very manly. He returned the little squeeze that tugged on his hand.

"Oh, I'm a big fellow," he answered.

"You look awful nice," the little girl pursued. "Just like one of my make-believe Princes. I wish you lived with Jimmie and me. I wouldn't mind Cynthia then."

"But the Princes never lived with the little girls in the stories, you know," argued Dale, finding it a very pleasant and unusual sensation to act the role of a Prince even to a very small girl. "You have to find me, you see."

Miss Robin jumped with joy. "Oh, goody, goody! I'll always make b'lieve you are a Prince and I'll find you and you must find me, too. You will, won't you?"

"You just bet I will," promised Dale, easily. "Here's your street." He stopped to study the house numbers. Suddenly a door flew open wide and a bareheaded man plunged into the street, almost tumbling upon them.

"Robin! Good gracious! I thought you were - stolen - lost -"

Robin, very calm, clasped him about his knee.

"I *was* lost, Jimmie. But this very big boy brought me home. He's a Prince - I mean he's my make-believe Prince."

"But, Robin -" The man turned from the child to Dale.

"I found her way down by Sheridan Square. She was hunting for her doll she'd left there."

"While I was walking with Mr. Tony this afternoon I played in the park and I forgot Cynthia."

"Good Heavens - and you went way off there all by yourself to find the thing?"

In her pride of Dale, Robin overlooked the slur on Cynthia.

"I went alone," she repeated, "but I came home with my Prince."

Gradually Robin's father was recovering from his shock. The muscles of his face relaxed; he ran his fingers through his thick hair, red like the child's, with a gesture of throwing off some horrible nightmare. To Dale he looked very boyish - with a little of Robin's own cherubic expression.

"Well, say, you gave me a fright, child. And you must promise not to do it again. Why, I can't ever leave you alone unless you do."

He turned to Dale, who stood, lingering, loath to leave the little Robin under the doubtful protection her Jimmie offered. "I'm no end grateful to you, my boy. If there's anything I can do for you -" He slipped one hand mechanically into his pocket.

"*I* don't want anything." Dale spoke curtly and stepped back. "It wasn't any bother; it's a nice night to walk."

With a child's quick intuition Robin realized that her gallant Prince was about to slip out of her sight. Her Jimmie had pulled his hand from his pocket and was extending it to the boy. He was not even inviting him to come in and smoke like he always invited Mr. Tony and Gerald and all the others. But of course Princes wouldn't smoke, anyway.

She waited until her father had finished his thanks, then, stepping up to Dale, she reached out two small arms and by holding on to Dale's, drew herself up almost to the boy's chin. Upon it she pressed a shy, warm kiss.

"Good-bye, Prince. You will hunt for me, won't you? Promise! Cross your heart!"

Dale, flaming red, confused, promised that he would, then wheeled and stalked off down the street. After he had rounded the corner he lifted his arm and wiped his chin with the sleeve of his coat. Then he stuck his hands deep in his pockets and whistled loudly. But after a moment, at a recollection of sky-blue eyes underneath a sky-blue tam-o'shanter, he chuckled softly. "A Prince! Gee, some Prince!" But his head instinctively went higher at the honor thrust upon him.

When he returned from the store, Dale usually found his mother sitting by the lamp crocheting. But tonight everything was different; scarcely had he stopped at their landing before the little mother, quite transformed, rushed to greet him and tell him the wonderful bit of good fortune.

Before it his own adventure was forgotten.

"And it's only a beginning it is - it's the superintendent he'll be in no time at all, at all," finished Mrs. Lynch.

"And we can move? And I can join the Boy Scouts? And go to camp next summer? And have a pair of roller skates?"

Mrs. Lynch nodded her head to each question. Behind each

note of her voice rippled a laugh. "Yes, yes, yes. Sure, it's a wonderful night this is."

"Where's Pop now?"

"Working with the extra shift," the wife answered, proudly.

"Any dumplings?" eagerly.

"And I was forgetting! Bless the heart of you, of course I saved the biggest. 'Twas like a party tonight for I dressed your sister in the beads. It's worn out she is, God love her, with the excitement and trying to keep her wee eyes open 'til her Pop come home. Hushee or you'll waken the lamb now."

Dale was deep in thought choosing the words with which he would tell the good news to the "fellows" on the morrow, his mother was busying herself with the "biggest" dumpling, when a peremptory knock came at the door. With a quick cry Mrs. Lynch dropped her spoon - why should anything intrude upon their joy this night?

A man stood on the threshold presenting a curious figure for he wore a heavy coat over a white duck suit. Where had she seen such a suit before? With a catch at her heart she remembered - at the hospital, that time Dale had been run over. "Oh!" she cried. "My Dan!"

"Mrs. Lynch?" The hospital attendant spoke quickly as one would who had a disagreeable task and must dispose of it without any delay. "Your husband's had an accident - he's alive, but - you'd better come."

Mrs. Lynch stood very still in the centre of the room - her hand clutching her throat as though to stifle the scream that tore it.

"My Dan - hurt!" She trembled but stood very straight. "Quick, Dale, we must go to him. My Dan. No, no, you stay with Beryl. Oh, *hurry!*" she implored the interne, rushing bareheaded past him down the stairway. "*Hurry.*"

For a few moments Dale stared at the half-open door. In his thirteen years he had experienced the pinch of poverty, even hunger, the pain of injury, but never this overwhelming fear of something, he did not know what. Pop, his big, strong Pop - hurt! Pop, who could swing him even now, that he measured five feet three himself, to his shoulder! Oh, no, no, it could not be true! Someone had made a mistake. Someone had cruelly frightened his mother. Hadn't their luck just come? Hadn't Pop been made a boss?

"Mom-ma!" came Beryl's voice, sleepily, from the other room. "Mom-ma, what's they?" Glad of anything to do Dale rushed to quiet his little sister. He bade her, brokenly, to "never mind and go to sleep," and he pulled the old blanket up tight to her chin, his eyes so blinded with tears that he did not see the waxen head pillowed close to Beryl's.

Then he sat in his mother's chair and dropped his head upon the table and waited, his hands clenched at his side.

"I *won't* cry! I *won't* be a baby! Mom'll maybe need me. I'm big now!" he muttered, finding a little comfort in the sound of his own voice.

* * * * *

Poor Robin's Prince; alas, he felt very young and helpless before the trouble which he faced.

Big Dan Lynch, he who had been the fairest and sturdiest of the county of Moira's girlhood, would never work again - as superintendent or even foreman; the rest of his days must be spent in the wheeled chair sent up by the sympathetic Miss Lewis of the Neighborhood Settlement House. It was fixed with a contrivance so that he could move it about the small room.

Jane Abbott

Little Beryl started school which made up for a great deal that had suddenly been taken from her life, for mother never sat by the lamp, now, or crocheted. She worked at the Settlement House all day and all evening busied herself with her home tasks.

The "lucky dolly" Beryl hid away in paper wrappings. Somehow, young as she was, she knew her mother could not bear the sight of it.

And Dale worked every day at Tony's, going to night school on the evenings when he had used to go to the store. A tightening about the lips, an older seriousness in the lad's eyes alone told what it had cost him to give up his ambition to graduate with his class, perhaps at its head.

Little Robin with the sky-blue eyes was quite forgotten!

CHAPTER III

THE HOUSE OF FORSYTH

It was a time-honored custom at Gray Manor that Harkness should serve tea at half-past four in the Chinese room.

On this day - another November day, ten years after the events of the last chapter - Harkness slipped through the heavy curtains with his tray and interrupted Madame Forsyth, mistress of Gray Manor, in deep confab with her legal advisor, Cornelius Allendyce.

Mr. Allendyce was just saying, crisply, "Will your mind not rest easier for knowing that the Forsyth fortune will go to a Forsyth?" when Harkness rattled the cups.

Then, strangest of all things, Madame ordered him sharply away with his tray.

Such a thing had never happened before in Harkness' experience and he had been at Gray Manor for fifty-five years. He grumbled complainingly to Mrs. Budge, the housekeeper, and to Florrie, Madame's own maid, who was having a sip of tea with Mrs. Budge in the cosy warmth of the kitchen.

Florrie asserted that she could tell them a story or two of Madame's whims and cranks - only it would not become her, inasmuch as Madame was old and a woman to be pitied. "Poor thing, with this curse on the house, who wouldn't have jumps and fidgets? I don't see I'm sure how any of us stand it." But Florrie spoke with a hint of satisfaction - as though proud to serve where there was a "curse." Harkness and Mrs. Budge, who had lived at Gray Manor when things were happier, sighed.

"It's an heir they be talking about now," Harkness admitted.

"You don't say so!" exclaimed Mrs. Budge and Florrie in one breath.

Up in the Chinese room Madame Forsyth was saying; "Do you think any child of that - branch of the family - could take the place of -"

"Oh, dear Madame," interrupted the lawyer. "I am not suggesting such a thing! I know how impossible that would be. But on my own responsibility I have made investigations and I have ascertained that your husband's nephew has the one child. The nephew's an artist of sorts and doubtless has his ups and downs - most artists do. Now I suggest -"

"That I take this - child -"

Mr. Allendyce tactfully ignored the scorn in her voice. "Exactly," he purred. "Exactly. Gordon is the child's name. A very nice name, I am sure."

"The child of an obscure artist -"

"Ah, but, Madame, blood is blood. A Forsyth -"

"P'ff!" Madame made a sound like rock hitting rock. Indeed, as she sat there, her narrow eyes gleaming from her immobile face, her thin lips tightly compressed, she looked much more like rock than flesh-and-blood.

Her explosion had the effect of exasperating the little lawyer out of his habitual attitude of conciliation.

"Madame, I can do no more than advise you in this matter. I have traced down this child as a possible heir to the Forsyth fortune. However, you have it in your power to will otherwise. But let me say this - not as a lawyer but as your friend. You are growing old. Will you not find, perhaps, more happiness in your old age, if you bring a little youth into this melancholy old house -"

"I must ask you to withhold your kind wishes until some other time," interrupted Madame, dryly. "I am at present seeking your advice as a lawyer. I have not been regardless of the fact that the House of Forsyth must have an heir; I have been thinking of it for a long time - in fact, that is all there is left for me to do. And, though it is exceedingly distasteful to me, I see the justice in seeking out one of - that family. But, it must be done in my way. My mind is quite made up to that. You say there is a - child. I wish you to communicate with this child's father - this relative of my husband, and inform him that I will make this child my heir provided he can be brought to Gray Manor at once. He will live for one year here under your guardianship. I will send for Percival Tubbs who, you may remember, tutored my grandson. Doubtless he is old-fogyish but from his long association with our family he knows the Forsyth traditions and what the head of the House of Forsyth should be. He will know whether this boy can be trained to measure up to it. If, after a year, he does not, he must go back - to his father. I will be fair, of course, as far as money goes. If he does -" She stopped suddenly, her stony demeanor broken. The thin lips quivered at the thought of that sunny south room in the great house where had been left untouched the toys, the books, the games, the precious trophies, the guns and racquets, golf sticks and gloves which marked each development of her beloved grandson.

"A very fair plan," murmured the lawyer.

"You have not heard all," went on Madame Forsyth in such a strange voice that Cornelius Allendyce looked up at her in astonishment. "I am going away."

"You! Where?" exclaimed the man. He could not quite believe his ears.

"That I do not care to divulge." She enjoyed his amazement. "I am yielding to a restlessness which in a younger woman you would understand, but which in me you would no doubt term - crazy. I am going to run away - to some new place, where, for awhile, no one will know whether I am the rich Madame Christopher Forsyth or the poor Mrs. John Smith. Oh, I shall be quite safe; at my bank they will be able to find me if anything happens. Norris has had entire charge of the mills for a long time. And Budge and Harkness can take care of things here."

"Madame," the lawyer was moved out of his customary reserve, "are you not possibly running away from what may bring you happiness - and comfort?"

For the space of a moment the real heart of the woman shone in her eyes.

"I *am* running away. I might learn to love this boy and he might not be what the head of the house of Forsyth *should* be and I would have to send him back. And my heart has been torn enough. It is tired. I have a whim to find new places - new things - to rest - and forget all this."

There was an interval of silence. Then Mr. Allendyce, lifting his eyes from the patent-leather tips of his shoes, said quietly:

"I will carry out your commands to the best of my ability."

There followed, then, a great deal of discussion over details. And, while carefully jotting figures and memoranda in a neat, morocco bound note-book, the little man of law felt as though he were writing the opening chapters of some fairy-tale.

Yet there was little of the fairy-tale in the old, empty house, a melancholy house in spite of its wealth of treasure, brought from every country on the globe. And there was nothing of romance in the Forsyth family which had come over to Connecticut from England in the early days of its settlement and had left to all the Forsyths to come, not only the beginnings of the Forsyth factory where thread was made by the millions of spools, and the Forsyth fortune, amassed by those same spools, but also a deal of that courage which had helped those pioneers endure the hardships and meet the obstacles of the early days.

Her business at an end, Madame expressed embarrassment at her inhospitality in denying Mr. Allendyce his cup of tea. Would he not stay and dine with her? Mr. Allendyce did not in the least desire to dine alone with his client but the Wassumsic Inn was an uninviting place and New York was a three hours' ride away. So he accepted with a polite show of pleasure and assured Madame that he could amuse himself in the library while she dressed for dinner.

Left to himself, the lawyer fell to pacing the velvety length of the library floor. This led him to one of the long windows. He stopped and looked out through it across the sloping lawns which surrounded the house. A low ribbon of glow hung over the edge of the hills which lay to the west of the town. Silhouetted against it was the ragged line of roofs and stacks which were the Forsyth Mills. Familiar with them through years of business association, the little man of law visualized them now as clearly as though they did not lay wrapped in evening shadow; he saw the ugly, age-old walls, the glaring brick of the new additions, the dingy yards, the silver thread of the river and across that the rows upon rows of tiny houses piled against one another, each like its neighbor even to the broken pickets surrounding squares of cinder ground. He knew, although his eyes could not see, that these yards even now were hung with the lines of everlasting washing, that men lounged on those back doorsteps and smoked and talked while women worked within preparing the evening meals. These human beings were machines in the gigantic industry upon which the House of Forsyth was founded. Did Madame ever think of them as flesh and blood mortals - like herself? Cornelius Allendyce smiled at the question; oh, no, the Forsyth tradition, of which Madame talked, built an impenetrable wall between her and those toilers.

Staring at the gray hard line of shadow that was the tallest of the chimneys the man thought how like it was to Madame and old Christopher Forsyth. His long connection with the family and the family interests gave the lawyer an intimate understanding of them and all that had happened to them. And it had been much. Mr. Allendyce himself often spoke of the "curse" of Gray Manor. Christopher Forsyth and Madame had had one son, Christopher Junior. Allendyce could recall the elaborate festivities that had marked the boy's coming of age, the almost royal pomp of his wedding. Three years after that wedding the young man and his wife had been drowned while cruising with friends off the coast of Southern California.

This terrible blow might have crushed old Christopher but for the toddling youngster who was Christopher the Third. The grandfather and grandmother shut themselves away in Gray Manor with the one purpose in life - to bring up Christopher the Third to take his place at the head of the House of Forsyth.

At this point in his reflections Mr. Allendyce's heart gave a quick throb of pity - he knew what that handsome lad had been to the old couple. He thought now how merciful it had been that old Christopher had died before that cruel accident on the football field in which the lad had been fatally injured. The brunt of the blow had fallen upon Madame. And after the boy's death, a gloom had settled over her and the old house which nothing had seemed able to dispel. As a last desperate resort the lawyer had suggested, with a courage that cost considerable effort, the finding of this other heir.

Mr. Allendyce had known very little of that "other branch" of the family. Old Christopher had had a younger half-brother, Charles, who, at the time Christopher took over the responsibilities of the head of the family, went off to South America where he married a young Spanish girl. And from the moment of that "low" marriage, as old Christopher had called it, to the investigation by Mr. Allendyce's agents, nothing had been heard at Gray Manor of this Charles Forsyth.

It had cost considerable money to trace him down but, accomplished, Mr. Allendyce had with satisfaction tabulated the results in his neat little note-book. Charles had died leaving one son, James. James had one child, Gordon. They lived at 22 Patchin Place, New York City.

The thought of the fairy story flashed back into the lawyer's mind. He knew his New York and he knew Patchin Place, where poverty and ambition elbowed one another, and squalor stabbed at the heart of beauty. This Gordon Forsyth had his childhood amid this, lived on the rise and fall of an artist's day-by-day fortune. Now he would be taken from all that, brought to Gray Manor, put under special tutorage, so that, some day he could step into that other lad's place. If that didn't equal an Arabian Night's tale!

"I'll go down to Patchin Place myself. I'd like to see their faces when I tell them!" he declared aloud, with a tingle within his heart that was a thrill although the little man did not know it.

Harkness coughed behind him. He turned quickly. Harkness bowed stiffly. "Madame awaits you in the drawing-room."

The little man-of-the-law's chin went out. "Madame awaits -" Poor old Madame; she would not have known how to come in and say "Let us go out to dinner." There had to be all the ceremony and fuss - or it would not have been Gray Manor and Madame Christopher Forsyth.

"All right. I'll find her," Mr. Allendyce growled. Then he was startled out of his usual composure by catching the suggestion of a twinkle in the Harkness eye which, of course, should not be in a Forsyth butler's eye at all.

CHAPTER IV

RED-ROBIN

For twenty-five years Cornelius Allendyce had worn nothing but black ties. On the morning of his contemplated invasion of Patchin Place in search of a Forsyth heir he knotted a lavender scarf about his neck and felt oddly excited. Such a sudden and unexplainable impulse, he thought, must portend adventure.

With a notion that all artists were "at home" at tea time, Mr. Allendyce waited until four o'clock before he approached his agreeable task. At the door of 22 Patchin Place he dismissed his taxicab and stood for a moment surveying the dilapidated front of the building - with a moment's mental picture of the magnificent pile that was Gray Manor.

A pretentious though slightly soiled register just inside the doorway, told him that "James Forsyth" lived on the fifth floor, so the little man toiled resolutely up the narrow, steep stairway, puffing as he ascended. It was necessary to count the landings to know, in the dimness of the hallway, when he reached the fifth floor. He had to pause outside the door to catch his breath; a moment's nausea seized him at the smell of stale food and damp walls.

But at his knock the door swung back upon so much sunshine and color that the little man blinked in amazement. A mite of a girl with a halo of sun-red hair smiled at him in a very friendly fashion.

"Does Mr. James Forsyth live here?" It seemed almost ridiculous to ask the question for surely it must be some witch's cranny upon which he had stumbled.

"Yes. But Jimmie isn't home. Won't you come in?"

Mr. Allendyce stared about the room - a big room, its size enhanced by the great glass windows and the glass skylight. Everywhere bloomed flowers in gayly painted boxes and pots and tubs. And after another blink Mr. Allendyce perceived that there were a few real chairs, very shabby, and a table covered with a cloth woven in brilliant colors and some very lovely pictures hanging wherever, because of the windows and the sloping roof, there was any place to hang them.

The young girl closed the door, whereupon there came a gay chirping from birds perching, the bewildered lawyer discovered, in various places around the room quite as though this corner of a tenement was a woodland.

"Hush, Bo, hush. They're dreadfully noisy. They love company. Won't you sit down?"

Mr. Allendyce sat gingerly upon the nearest chair. His companion pulled one up close to him. He perceived with something of a shock that she limped and at this discovery he looked at her again and drew in a quick breath.

Why, here was the oddest little thing he had ever seen. He had thought her a child, yet the wide eyes, set deep and of the blue of midnight, had a quaint seriousness and understanding; in the corner of her lips lingered a tender droop oddly at variance with the childish dimple of the finely moulded chin. Though the girl's red hair - like flame, as the lawyer had first thought, gave her an alive look, the little form under the queer straight dress was diminutive to frailty.

"Who are you, my dear?"

"Robin Forsyth. Jimmie calls me Red-Robin because I hop when I walk."

"Is Jimmie your -"

"He's my Parent. Do you know Jimmie?"

"N-no, not - exactly." The little man was wondering how his investigators had failed to report this young girl.

"Jimmie ought to be here soon. He went out to sell a picture to old Mrs. Wycke. She wanted it but she wanted it cheap, Jimmie says. But we didn't have anything to eat today so he took the picture to her and he's going to bring back some cake and ice cream. We'll have a party. Will you stay?"

"Good heavens," thought Allendyce, startled at her astonishing frankness. He reached out and patted the small hand.

"You are very kind. Does your Jimmie sell - many pictures?"

"Not many - I heard him and Mr. Tony talking. Mr. Tony's his best friend. If it were not for me Jimmie'd go away with Mr. Tony. Mr. Tony writes, you see, and he wants Jimmie to illustrate for him."

"And where is your brother Gordon?"

Robin stared. "My - brother - Gordon?"

"Yes. Gordon -"

"*I* am Gordon."

"You!"

"My real name is Gordon but Jimmie doesn't like it. He always said it was too formal for a little girl. So he calls me Red-Robin and he says he'll never call me anything else. Why do you look so funny?"

For Mr. Allendyce seemed to have crumpled together and to be quite speechless.

"Don't *you* think I'm too, oh, sort of insignificant, to be Gordon? I like Robin much better."

The lawyer did not hear her. Here was a fine balking of all his and Madame's plans. The Forsyth heir! That that heir should be a girl had never entered their calculations. And a little lame girl at that; Mr. Allendyce suddenly recalled how Madame had worshipped the splendid manliness of young Christopher the Third.

"Is there anything the matter with you, Mr. - why, you haven't told me your name!"

With a tremendous effort Cornelius Allendyce pulled himself together. He flushed under the wondering wide-eyed scrutiny of his companion, who reached out and laid a small, warm hand upon his.

"You're not ill, are you?" with solicitude.

"No - no, my dear. No, I am not ill. But I am upset. You see - I came here - well, I call it - a most interesting story. Up in Connecticut there's a small town and a very big mill which has been there for ever so long, heaping up millions of dollars. And there's a very big house there that looks like a castle because it's built of gray stone and is up on a hill - it has everything but the moat itself. And an old lady lives there all alone." The lawyer paused, a little frightened at a wild thought that was persistently creeping up over his sensibilities. It must be the lavender tie or the witchery of the flowers and the absurd chirping birds.

"Oh, that's the old Dragon!" cried Robin, delightedly, with a chuckle as though she knew all about the old lady and the

Jane Abbott

lonely castle. "That's what Jimmie calls her - poor old thing. Jimmie says she must be dreadfully unhappy in that lonely old house after all that's happened there."

"Do you - do you mean that - you *know* -"

"About those rich Forsyth's? Why, of course. That's Jimmie's pet story - about his terrible relatives."

"But your father has never -"

"Seen her? Oh, no. Jimmie's very proud, you see. And he thinks one good picture is worth more than any old fortune or mill or anything. Oh, Jimmie's wonderful. Why, we wouldn't trade our little home here for two of her castles! Jimmie couldn't paint if he were rich. He says money kills genius. Only -" She stopped abruptly, flushing.

"Only what, my dear -"

"I ought not to rattle on like this to you. Jimmie says I am - sometimes - *too* friendly. I suppose it's because I don't know many people. But I wish I just had a *little* money. You see *I'm* not a bit of a genius. I can't paint like Jimmie or sing like my mother did - or do a single thing."

Now Mr. Allendyce suddenly felt so excited that he wriggled on the rickety chair until it creaked threateningly.

"If you had money, Miss Gordon - what would you do?"

"Why I'd run away." She answered with startling promptness. "Oh, I don't mean that I'm not happy here. I love it. And I adore Jimmie. But I'm a girl and I'm lame, so I'm a - a millstone 'round Jimmie's neck!"

"What in the world -"

"*Promise* you won't ever tell him what I'm saying. Oh, he'd feel dreadfully. You see it's just that. He feels sorry 'cause I'm lame and he won't believe that I don't mind a bit - why, I can run and do everything - and he won't ever go anywhere without me. And an artist shouldn't have to be tied down; I heard Mr. Tony say so, once, when Jimmie was very blue. He didn't know I heard. Now Mr. Tony's going off for a long cruise in the South Seas on a sailing boat and he wants Jimmie to go with him. He's going to write stories and he says if Jimmie sees it all he will make his fortune painting pictures. And he can illustrate the stories, too. And Jimmie won't go because he won't leave me. Don't you see what I'd do if I had some money? I'd run away somewhere and tell Jimmie that he must go with Mr. Tony."

Mr. Allendyce sprang to his feet and paced up and down the room. In all his life the world had never seemed so full of youth and color and adventure as it did at that precise moment; his cautious soul fairly burst with imaginative daring.

"Miss Gordon - that's what I came for. I mean, I came to tell this Gordon Forsyth that the old lady, Madame Forsyth, wanted him to come to Gray Manor to live - for a year. He's to be tutored there. And if at the end of a year he is a -"

"But there isn't any he! Gordon's me."

"I know. I know. But a Forsyth's a Forsyth."

"You mean - *I* might go to - the castle -"

"Yes, why not? Madame - and I - just took it for granted that you were a boy, because of your name. But our mistake does not make you any less a Forsyth or less a possible heir -" The thought was a full-fledged idea now!

"Who *are* you?" broke in Robin, excitedly.

"I am Cornelius Allendyce, attorney for the Forsyth family.

Jane Abbott

And I am - if your father consents - your future guardian."

"Oh, Jimmie'll *never* consent, never!"

"Why not?" pressed the lawyer. "You say you have no - particular genius to be killed by - money."

"Would it mean that I'd have to give Jimmie up forever?"

"No, my dear. Indeed no. Madame's plan is that you are to go to Gray Manor under my guardianship to live for a year. At the end of that time, if she is satisfied - Why, your father would simply give up any claim -"

"Oh, you don't know Jimmie. He'd never do it, unless -" she paused, her eyes suddenly wet, "unless - *I* - gave *him* up. All his life he's made sacrifices and given up things for me - big chances. So now - couldn't I run away with you - and then write and tell him?"

The Cornelius Allendyce who had lived up to that moment of crossing the threshold of this fifth-floor witchery would have scorned such a suggestion as "ridiculous! ridiculous!" But the Cornelius Allendyce of the lavender tie saw mad possibilities in such a step. Take the girl to Gray Manor and settle with Mr. James Forsyth afterwards.

"Couldn't I?"

"Why - yes, if you think your father would accept the situation - when he knew."

"Oh, I'd tell him he *had* to, that he must go away with Mr. Tony. And he'd go. But, Mr. Allendyce - I couldn't go tonight. I just couldn't let Jimmie come back with the ice cream and cake and maybe a pumpkin pie and - not find me here. Our parties are such fun. If you'll come tomorrow at three o'clock - I'll be ready. But what will the Dragon say when she sees that I'm a girl?"

Mr. Allendyce suddenly laughed aloud. The whole thing was so very simple. Madame only waited a telegram from him to set forth upon her travels. Why let her know that Gordon was a girl until the year had passed?

"We will not worry about that, my dear. Madame is going away. She will not be back at Gray Manor for a long time. I will call at three - tomorrow. I trust you will make your Jimmie understand. You know this is a very unusual step - there are some who might call it abduction -"

"Oh, Jimmie wouldn't!" assured Robin. "Not when I tell him why I'm running away."

Robin had answered him so indifferently that Cornelius Allendyce felt her mind was working out a plan for the morrow. He gave a last look about the room as though he wished to carry away a perfect impression of it, then patted the girl on the shoulder.

"Here is my card and the telephone number of my office. If you decide that this step is - too irregular, if perhaps we ought to talk with your father first -"

"No! No!" cried Robin. "That would spoil everything!"

Down in the street Cornelius Allendyce waved off a persistent taxi driver, deciding that he needed the vent of exercise to bring him back to earth. And as he hurried along he felt a curious elation, as though for the first time he enjoyed a zest in living. As a lawyer his life had been necessarily cut-and-dried; there had been little room for adventuring. And now, in a brief half-hour, he had let himself into the wildest sort of conspiracy. (He stopped suddenly and mopped his forehead.) He was planning to deliberately deceive Madame Forsyth, to steal a young and very unusual girl from her parent - and, to assume the guardianship of this same runaway. Where would it all end?

Jane Abbott

But in that half-hour just past something must have happened to the little man's conscience for even after the startling summing up, he laughed and walked on with a step lighter than before.

*   *   *   *   *

Back on the fifth floor of the old house in Patchin Place Robin leaned over the table writing a letter. Her task was made the more difficult because of the tears which blinded her eyes.

"Jimmie, I love you more than anything in the world but I am going to run away and leave you. I am going to the Dragon. She wants an heir. I am going to live in the castle and have a tutor. And my guardian is going to be the Dragon's lawyer - he's ever so nice and fathery - so you see I will be looked after as well as can be. Jimmie dearest-darling, you must not worry about me or try to make me come back for I'll be all right and you must go away with Mr. Tony and paint lots and I'll be so proud. And please, please Jimmie, make Aunt Milly promise to take care of the birds and the flowers for they mustn't die. And you will write to me, won't you? Good-bye, Jimmie, don't forget your hot milk at night. Yours always and always, Red-Robin."

She had just signed the letter when James Forsyth opened the door. She thrust it into her pocket as she turned to meet him.

"Oh, *Jimmie*!" she cried, for under his arm he carried the picture he had taken to sell to Mrs. Wycke.

"She didn't want it," he explained, testily.

The girl had been well schooled in disappointment; not the slightest shadow now crossed her face.

"*Someone* will, Jimmie," she declared, brightly, taking the heavy package from him. "And you said yourself Mrs. Wycke couldn't tell a chromo from a masterpiece. We don't want her to have our picture anyway. I'm not a bit hungry - are you, Jimmie? Let's sit here all cosy and you read to me -" and thinking of the note that lay in her pocket, she reached up very suddenly and kissed her Jimmie to hide the break in her voice.

CHAPTER V

JIMMIE

Robin found running away amazingly simple. Poor Jimmie, at her urging, went out quite unsuspecting. She was so excited and there was so much to be done at the last moment, that she had no time to think what the parting with all she loved so dearly must mean to her.

Promptly at three o'clock Cornelius Allendyce tapped on the door. His face was very red and moist and his hand, as he reached out for Robin's bag, shook, but Robin did not notice all that; she slipped quickly through the door and shut it behind her, as though fearful that at the last moment she might find it impossible to go.

Out in the thin sunshine, whirring through the traffic of the crowded streets, neither spoke for breathlessness. Cornelius Allendyce stared at the buildings and swallowed at regular intervals to steady his nerves - a trick he had always found most helpful in important legal trials. Robin kept her eyes glued on the back of the taxi driver's head but he might have had two heads and one upside down for all she noticed. Her hands in her lap were clenched very tight and her lips were pressed in a straight, thin, resolute line.

But as they kept on past Forty-second street and headed toward Central Park West the lawyer explained that he was taking her to his own home for the night.

"My sister will make you quite comfortable. Tomorrow we will go out to Wassumsic." He did not say that it was important, too, to give Madame Forsyth ample opportunity to get away from Gray Manor.

Robin drew a long breath and relaxed. It had taken so very much courage to run away that she had little left with which to face her new life. Tomorrow it might be easier.

Miss Effie Allendyce took her under her wing in a fluttery, mothery sort of a way with a great many "my dear's."

"I suppose," the lawyer had said, looking at the two, "you, Effie, will have to get Miss Forsyth some clothes tomorrow -"

"Clothes," Robin cried, astonished. "I - brought some."

"Well, you probably ought to have some other kind. You see, my dear, you are a Forsyth of Gray Manor now." He turned to his sister. "Effie, can you get all she needs - everything, before tomorrow at three o'clock?"

Effie's eyes danced at such a task - indeed, she could. She knew a shop where she could buy everything that a girl might need.

"Well, I'll leave you two to make out lists. Isn't that what you have to do?"

So, for a few hours the making of these amazing lists kept Robin's thoughts from that little fifth floor home and Jimmie. Miss Effie began with shoes and finished with hats, with little abbreviations in brackets to include caps and scarfs and all sorts of things. "It is very cold in Wassumsic," she explained, "and you will live a great deal out of doors. It is very lovely," she added, making a round period after "sweater."

And there was another list which included a wrist watch and a writing set. "They can send on most of these things," she pondered.

Robin slyly pinched herself to know that she was still a living-breathing girl; all seemed as unreal as though she had slipped away into a magician's world.

But the lists completed, dinner over, alone with her new guardian, an overwhelming loneliness swept her. Cornelius Allendyce, turning from a protracted study of the blazing fire, was startled to find the girl's head pillowed in her arm, her shoulders shaking with smothered sobs.

"My dear! My dear!" he exclaimed, very much as Miss Effie would have done.

"I - I can't help it. I tried -"

Poor Robin looked so very small in the big chair that remorse seized Cornelius Allendyce. How could he have taken this little girl from her corner, shabby as it was?

It was not too late -

"Miss Gordon," he began a little uneasily, wondering what guardians did when their wards were hysterical. "My dear, don't cry, I beg of you. Come, it is not too late to go back. We will explain -"

Robin lifted her head. "I - I don't want to go back. But I was thinking of Jimmie. He must be awfully lonesome - now. You see you don't know Jimmie. He depends on me to remind him of things like his hot milk. And just at first, it will be hard. But, no, no, I don't want to go back."

"Then I would suggest that you go to bed. You are doubtless very tired from the excitement of everything. And tomorrow will be a busy day - and an interesting day."

Robin drew herself slowly from the chair. She limped over to the divan upon which Cornelius Allendyce sat. Her eyes were very steady, dark with earnestness.

"I'm ashamed I cried. I won't do it again. But I want you to know, oh, you must know, that I'm not going to Gray Manor because of all those clothes and the money or anything like that. There could not be anything at Gray Manor as nice as Jimmie's and my bird-cage. But I want Jimmie to have his chance -"

Left alone, Cornelius Allendyce found himself haunted by Robin's "Jimmie must be awfully lonesome." What a strange pair - the quaint old-young girl living in a world which circled around this father - the father, by the girl's own assertion, "depending" upon the girl. And little Robin, scarcely more than a child, realizing that she hindered the man's development, talking about giving him "his chance" and at such cost - and promising that she would not cry again. "There's bravery for you!" muttered the lawyer aloud.

He believed that Miss Effie's lists of finery and knick-knacks held little attraction for the girl.

He recalled Madame Forsyth's scornful "that other branch of the family." Yet this James Forsyth and Gordon had lived for years and often in want in New York City, and had never approached Madame for as much as a penny. Robin had said Jimmie couldn't paint if he were rich. Could he paint if he lost her?

Suddenly Cornelius Allendyce had a vivid understanding of the tie that bound these two. And it was unthinkable that this man would let the girl go and do nothing. Yet it was not of any possible embarrassment *he* might suffer that Cornelius Allendyce thought at this moment; it was of the heartbreak of the father. He had not considered him at all; carried away by a mad impulse he had let himself listen to a child and had lost his own sense of justice. Why, it had been rank robbery! He must go to this man at once. Muttering to himself he went in search of his hat and coat.

*   *   *   *   *

For the third time the little lawyer climbed the flights of stairs at 22 Patchin Place. And this time, so eager was he to square himself with Robin's Jimmie, he ran up the steps. He knocked twice and when no one answered he opened the door quietly and walked in.

A man sat at the little table, his head dropped in his outflung arms. Cornelius Allendyce knew it was Jimmie. Another man stood over him, his face flushed with impatience. "Mr. Tony," thought the lawyer. He was evidently just drawing breath after a heated argument.

"Pardon my intrusion, gentlemen. I knocked but I do not think you heard me." Allendyce stopped short, for his usual measured words seemed out of place at this moment. "I am Cornelius Allendyce," he finished humbly and guiltily. "I came back to - explain."

James Forsyth made a lightning-quick movement as though he would spring at the little lawyer's throat. Mr. Tony held him back.

"Jimmie - wait. Let him talk."

"It was Miss Robin's wish to slip away without telling you. She said you would not let her go and she had quite made up her mind to give you - what she calls - your chance. She has an idea that she ties you down -"

Jimmie choked as a sob strangled in his throat. His anger suddenly melted to abjection. Mr. Tony laid a comforting hand on his shoulder and turned to the lawyer.

"The girl is right. She's a wonderful little thing. She always could see further ahead than her Dad. I have been telling my pal that this is the best thing all around that could happen - a fine bit of luck for everyone. Robin will go up to Gray Manor and be as happy and safe as can be and her father can travel and work - the way Robin wants him to. Robin took rather unusual means to gain her end but - well, she knew what she was doing."

Jimmie turned to Cornelius Allendyce and studied his face with a desperate keenness.

"She isn't like other children," he began slowly. "Poor little crooked kiddie. She's sensitive. I've kept her away from everything that could hurt her. I've tried - to make up to her. I thought she was happy; I did not know she guessed - or knew -"

Mr. Tony had taken a few steps down the room. He wheeled now and came back with a set expression on his face as though he had to say something disagreeable and must get it over with.

"Jimmie, suppose, just for once, you look your soul straight in the eye - honest. Now isn't it the artist heart of you that's hurt by Robin's crooked little body - and not the child? Don't you keep her shut up in here because, when people stare at her - *you* suffer? Have you been fair to her? Oh, yes - you love her, all right. Well, then, let her go. Robin thinks she's giving you your chance - well, *I* say, give the girl her own."

"I tell you Robin's different - she doesn't want money or clothes!"

"Well, pretty things - and good food - can make even a 'different' girl's heart lighter. Come, old man, go off with me on this cruise and work your head off and at the end of the year - if Robin's not happy there, well, you can make other plans. I'm like Robin, I believe that give you a year, you'll do something rather big."

James Forsyth suddenly lifted a face so boyishly helpless, so defeated, that Allendyce's heart went out to him. He understood, all at once, what little Robin had meant when she had said, "You don't know Jimmie!" He certainly was not like other men.

"I feel such a - quitter. I promised Robin's mother - I'd make up to the child for her being lame - the way *she* would have, if she'd lived. And I've failed. Why, only last night she went to bed hungry." There followed a moment of tense silence, then the man went on dully, in a tone that implied yielding. "I suppose I may know all the circumstances that led up to - this."

Cornelius Allendyce proceeded to tell everything from the day of his interview with Madame to the moment of his consternation upon discovering that Gordon Forsyth was a girl and not a boy. He repeated word for word Robin's and his conspiring; he described their flight and Robin's break down in his library.

"She had not lost courage - oh, no. But she was thinking of you. She was afraid you'd forget to take your hot milk at night or something like that," he finished simply.

There were other details for the lawyer to explain to James Forsyth, having to do with allowances and schooling. Then, when everything had been said that was necessary to be said, James Forsyth rose wearily.

"If that's all, I'd like it if you two would leave me here - alone." He held out his hand to Mr. Allendyce. "Understand, if she's not happy -"

"Our agreement ends."

CHAPTER VI

THE FORSYTH HEIR

Harkness' mother had once lived in an English duke's family and Harkness had been brought up on stories of the ceremonious life there. Therefore he considered it quite fitting that he should take upon himself the planning for the reception of the Forsyth heir.

"I say it do be a pity Madame could not 'ave waited," he grumbled to Mrs. Budge. "To 'ave the poor little fellow arrive here alone don't seem right. But Madame says 'Harkness, you'll do everything - '"

"Everything!" snorted Mrs. Budge, who had just come down from dusting the "boy's" room. The familiar "clutter," as she had always called it, had roused poignant memories, so that her wrinkled face was streaked now and red. "'Pears to me most you do is talk - and talk big. It's Harkness this and Harkness that! To be sure *my* mother was a plain New England woman -"

"Now, Budge, now, Budge," interrupted Harkness, consolingly. "No one as I know is going to dispute that your mother was a plain New England woman. And we're not going to quarrel at such a rememberable moment, not we. And we're going to give Mr. Gordon a welcome as is befitting a Forsyth. At the appointed hour we'll gather at the door - you must stand at the head of the long line of servants -"

"Long line of servants! And where do you expect to get them, I'd like to know? Things have been at sixes and sevens in this house ever since the gloom came. And that new piece from the village ain't worth her salt's far as work goes."

Poor Harkness had to recognize the truth of what Budge said. Since the "gloom" things *had* been going at sixes and sevens - inexperienced help called up from the village to fill any need. He was not to be daunted, however; there were the gardener and the undergardener and the chauffeur and the stableman and they had wives who might be induced to put on their Sunday clothes and join in the ceremonial - all in all, they could make a fair showing.

Into the plans for the dinner Mrs. Budge threw herself with her whole heart. There must be young turkey and cranberry sauce, and a tasty salad and a good old New England pumpkin pie, which she would make herself, and ice cream and little cakes with colored frosting - oh, Budge knew what a boy liked.

And Harkness would brighten the great dark hall with bitter-sweet and deck the gloomy rooms with flowers - he knew what was proper for the coming of the heir of the House of Forsyth.

"Like as not," Budge said, "'twill be the end to this curse."

So the two old retainers, their hearts full of hope for a new happiness over Gray Manor, labored until the old house shone and bloomed for the coming of Gordon Forsyth. And a few minutes before the hour of arrival, the gardener and the undergardener and the stableman and their wives came in, breathless with importance; Chloe, the old colored cook, appeared in a brand new turban and 'kerchief. Mrs. Budge, her gray hair brushed back tighter than ever, donned her black silk which she had not worn since young Christopher's eighteenth birthday and took her place at the head of the line just a foot or two behind Harkness who, of course, had the honor of opening the door.

Mrs. Budge, however, watched the service door at the end of the long hall with fretful eyes. "That piece," she confided to Harkness, the moment not being so important as to still her grumbling, "said she wouldn't come in. And when I told her she could just choose t'wixt this and the door she said she wouldn't dress up, anyways. Impertinent chit! Thinks she's too good for the place. Things *have* gone to sixes and sevens -"

Harkness was holding his watch in his hand. And just as he shut it with a significant click, a tall dark-haired girl in a plain gingham dress slipped into the room and took her place at the end of the line, at the same moment casting a defiant glance at the knot which adorned the back of Mrs. Budge's head.

Above the low murmur of voices came the throb of a motor.

"It's him!" cried Harkness, a catch in his voice. Mrs. Budge shut her eyes tight from sheer nervousness. There was a visible straightening and a rustling of the line. Then Harkness threw the door open and bent low.

On the threshold stood a small girl; her eyes, under the fringe of red hair, wide with excitement, frightened.

Harkness had opened his lips for his little speech of welcome but the first sound died with a cackle in his throat, leaving his mouth agape. He stared at the little creature and beyond her at Cornelius Allendyce, who was superintending the unloading of several bags and boxes.

Where was Gordon Forsyth?

Turning, Mr. Allendyce, at one glance, took in the situation. He bustled up the steps, and thrust a bag in Harkness' limp hand.

"Well, we're here!" he cried cheerily, ignoring the amazement and disappointment that fairly tingled in the air. "And a fine welcome you're giving us!" He turned to Robin, who stood rooted to the threshold. "My dear, these people have served the Forsyths faithfully and for a long time. Harkness, this is Gordon Forsyth. Mrs. Budge -"

He drew aside to let Robin enter. And Robin, conscious of startled, curious eyes upon her, limped into her new home. Harkness, because he had to do something, closed the door slowly behind her.

"I'm sure - we were expecting -" he mumbled.

Mr. Allendyce imperiously waved off whatever Harkness was expecting.

"We hope, Mrs. Budge, you are prepared for two hungry people. We lunched very early and the ride here is always tiresome. In Madame's absence, I am sure you will take care of Miss Gordon and - me." There was the finest inflection on the "miss." "I shall stay a day or two. Robin, my dear, this is your new home."

Robin had been biting her lips to keep them steady. There was something so terrible in the great hall, the broad stair that lost itself in a cavern of darkness above, the brilliant lights, the staring faces. Her eyes swept from Mrs. Budge's stony face down the line and crossed the curious glance of the dark-haired girl in the gingham dress. Robin's brightened, for the girl was young, but the girl flushed a dark red, tossed her head and stalked through the narrow service door out of the room.

Robin turned to Cornelius Allendyce and clung to his arm. He seemed the one nice friendly thing in the whole place. And, as though he knew how she felt, he patted her hand in a way that seemed to say, "Courage, my dear."

Mrs. Budge recovered her tongue. "She'll not be wanting the young *master's* room," she said crisply. "Madame's orders -"

"I would suggest that Miss Gordon decide for herself what

room she will have." The lawyer's voice carried a rebuke that was not lost upon the housekeeper. "Harkness, carry the bags upstairs and Miss Gordon and I will follow."

So Harkness' reception line broke up; the gardener and the undergardener and their wives following Mrs. Budge's stiff back out through the service door while Harkness led Robin and her new guardian up the broad stairway.

In the kitchen, for very want of strength, Mrs. Budge flopped into a chair.

"Sixes and sevens!" she gasped. "I'll say that things *are* just going to sixes and sevens. I've always distrusted all lawyer-men and this one ain't a bit different. Bringing a *girl* here, and a cripple. Did you ever hear the like?" She looked from one to the other of Harkness' retainers and answered herself with the same breath. "You never did. Don't know when I've been so flabbergasted. Mebbe she's a Forsyth but she ain't a worthwhile Forsyth. She ain't. As if a girl could step into our boy's shoes." She sniffed audibly. "She don't take in Hannah Budge."

When Harkness appeared there was a fresh outburst and a reiteration that Hannah Budge "wasn't going to be taken in by a piece no bigger'n a pint of cider."

"Well, the girl's here - and hungry," Harkness retorted with meaning abruptness.

A sense of duty never failed to spur poor Budge. She rose, now, quickly. "Humph, like as not with everything else going to sixes and sevens that old Chloe's forgot her turkey," and with a heavy sigh that fairly rattled the stiff silk on her bosom she went off in search of the cook.

Robin found much difficulty in choosing her room for they all seemed equally lovely in the perfection of their furnishings. She had stood for a moment in the door of the south room that had been Christopher the Third's. "Here's where they'd have put you if you were a boy," her new guardian had told her. In spite of Mrs. Budge's efforts at cleaning and dusting, a melancholy hung over the room and about all the boyish things there was such a sense of waiting that Robin was glad to turn away. Finally she decided upon a west room the windows of which overlooked the valley and the hills beyond.

"Oh, wouldn't Jimmie love that?" she had cried, lingering in one of the windows. "He loves hills, and doesn't that river look like a silver ribbon tying the brown fields?"

The bedroom opened on one side into a sitting room with a bay window, on the other into a tiny bathroom, shining and gleaming with nickel and tile.

"Oh, everything's *lovely*," and Robin ecstatically clasped her hands. "Only what'll I ever do with everything so big!"

Cornelius Allendyce laughed at her dismay. To be sure he had not spent his life in such tiny quarters as the bird cage and he could not understand the girl's state of mind.

"My dear, after a little everything will seem quite natural. And remember - everything is at your command. This is your home. You are Gordon Forsyth. You will not have time to be lonely."

Robin's serious face suddenly broke into a bright smile. She patted the garland of roses which held back the silk hangings.

"I just had the funniest feeling, as if I were not me at all but all of a sudden someone else. Ever since I was a very little girl I've often played that I lived a make-believe story - I make it like all the fairy stories jumbled together. And I fit all the people I know into the different characters. Jimmie lets me play it because I am alone so much and it keeps me happy. Sometimes he even plays it with me. It makes horrid things seem nice. And Jimmie never wanted me to know the boys and girls at school - because I'm lame, I guess - so I always pretended things about them and gave them names. You should have seen Bluebeard." She laughed at the recollection. "And now I'm going on playing. I'm the little beggar-maid who awakens to find her self in the castle. Do you suppose there's a fairy godmother somewhere? And - a prince?"

And Cornelius Allendyce who had never read a fairy story in his life, let alone acted one, laughed with her.

"Yes, this is another chapter in your story."

"Oh, and don't you wish we could just peek to the end and see how it all turns out? But that isn't fair. And we couldn't - anyway."

Her new guardian shook his head. "No, we couldn't - anyway."

CHAPTER VII

BERYL

A bell tinkling somewhere in the house wakened Robin the next morning. Through the flowered chintz curtains of her window the sun shone with a warmth out of all keeping with the time of the year, throwing such a joyous glow about everything in the room that she rubbed her eyes to be sure she was not dreaming.

The evening before, everything had seemed so strange that Robin had not been able to take in small things; now an immense curiosity to explore Gray Manor, and the grounds that were like Central Park, and the little town, and the hills around it, seized her. She slipped her feet out of bed and into the satin slippers which had been one of Miss Effie's purchases. She dressed with feverish haste, rebuking herself for having slept so late, for her new wrist watch told her it was after ten o'clock.

Ten o'clock - why, on Patchin Place the morning was almost over at that hour, the streets about thundering with the work of the day. And here it was as still as night, or as - a church on a weekday, Robin thought.

Dressed, she opened the door of her room very quietly and peeped curiously out. And there in the wide hall, dusting an old highboy, was the girl with the dark hair.

"Hullo!" exclaimed Robin, delighted at the encounter.

The girl stared for a moment. She was tall and thin; her eyes so intensely blue as to look black and startling in their contrast to the whiteness of her skin. They were brooding, smoldering eyes and a too frequent scowl was making tiny lines between the straight black eyebrows.

"Isn't this the wonderfulest morning?" Robin advanced, stepping nearer. "What is your name? I'm Robin - I mean Gordon Forsyth."

"I know that. My name's Beryl but I guess it doesn't make much difference to you what I'm called. The man who came with you's waiting downstairs."

In spite of this rebuff Robin lingered for a moment, hopeful of a pleasanter word. But the girl Beryl shouldered her duster and marched off, head high.

"I'm going to find out more about her right off," determined Robin as she went in search of her guardian.

The big rooms below, like her own room, looked very different in the morning light, even cheery. Mr. Allendyce greeted her with a smile and Harkness' "Good-morning, Miss Gordon," had pleasant warmth. It was fun to sit in the high-backed chair before the shining silver and the flowers and to choose between grapefruit and frosted orange juice. So fascinated was Robin that she forgot for the time, her interest in the girl she had encountered upstairs.

"Well, what do you think of Gray Manor in daylight?" asked Mr. Allendyce as the two walked into the library.

"Oh, it's more like a great castle than ever. But it isn't - half as bad as I thought it was." When Robin caught the amused twinkle in her guardian's eye she added hastily: "I mean, it isn't gloomy and sad at all. It's so beautiful - and I love

Jane Abbott

beautiful things."

Mr. Allendyce thought suddenly that it was the first time for a long time *he* had seen these rooms when they had not seemed overhung with melancholy. But he checked any expression of the thought; instead he took Robin on a tour through the library and drawing rooms, pointing out to her the treasures which had been brought from every corner of the world. There were rare tapestries and bronzes, and tiny ivory carvings and tables inlaid with bright jade and old crystal candelabra, and quaint chests and wonderful paintings and rare old books. As he told the story of each, Cornelius Allendyce marvelled at the girl's quick appreciation and intelligent interest. Her Jimmie had evidently gathered travelled people about him and Robin had been always a sharp listener.

Then Harkness interrupted their pleasant occupation by appealing to Robin for "his orders" with such a comical solemnity that Robin had difficulty suppressing a nervous giggle. Her guardian came to her rescue with the suggestion that they drive about the town and the mills, have an early tea and an early dinner and dispense with luncheon.

"Must I tell him every day just what I want?" thought Robin, in dismay.

The girl's active imagination could well picture the imposing motor which came to the door as a coach-and-four, resplendent with regal trappings. And, cuddled in the wolf-skin robes, flying over the frosty roads which wound through the hills, it was very easy to feel like a princess from one of her own stories.

Only the mills spoiled her lovely day. The evening before they had loomed obscurely and interestingly but in broad daylight they were ugly. The great chimneys belched black smoke into the beautiful blue of the sky; the monotonous drone of many machines jarred the hillside quiet. Everything was so dusty and dirty - even the tiny houses where the men lived. Robin, brought up though she had been in Patchin Place, turned in disgust from the dreary ugliness about her.

"Does it have to be like that?" she asked her guardian.

"Like what?"

"Oh - dirty. And so dreary. And noisy."

Her guardian laughed. "I'm afraid it does. Work is mostly always drab - like that. And you see it has grown like a giant. There - there's the giant for your fairy story, my dear. And giants are usually ugly, aren't they?"

"Yes, always." Robin spoke with conviction. As they rode on she looked back over her shoulder. "I'm glad we can't stop today. This ride has been so lovely that I'd hate to spoil it by - seeing the Giant up close."

"Giants are very powerful. And usually very rich." Cornelius Allendyce enjoyed the fancy.

"Yes - and they crush and kill, too."

"But didn't a Jack climb something or other and overcome one of them in his lair?"

At this Robin laughed and then forgot, for the time being, the mills and the dirty houses; when Mr. Allendyce hoped Mrs. Budge would give them a very big tea party, she realized she was hungrier than she had ever been before.

So full had been each moment of her first day at Gray Manor that it was not until she sat curled in the big divan before the library fire, a book of colored plates of Italian gardens across her lap that she thought of her determination to know more of the girl who had called herself Beryl.

Harkness stood at the long table putting it in order. Harkness

Jane Abbott

seemed always moving things about just so as to put them back in place again.

"Mr. Harkness."

"Yes, Miss Gordon."

"Do I know everybody here?"

"Why - I'm sure - What do you mean, Miss Gordon?"

"I saw a young girl last night. And I met her in the hall today. Who's she?"

"That's a person from the village, Miss Gordon. I don't know as I've heard her name. Budge mostly calls her a piece. I don't think Budge is satisfied with her."

"You mean she works here?"

"Yes, Miss Gordon. At least now. She helps Budge. Budge is getting on, you see. I don't know as I've heard the miss' name. Is there anything more, Miss Gordon?"

Harkness had a warm heart under his faded livery and it went out now to Robin because she looked very small and very much alone in the big room. He had heard Mrs. Budge's hostile sputter and he knew the lawyer man was going the next day; little Miss Gordon would be quite without friends at Gray Manor. So he stepped closer to the divan and in a very human, friendly way he added: "Excuse me if I'm so bold as to say, you just count on old Harkness if you want anything, missy."

Robin caught the kindliness in the man's voice. "Oh, thank you, Mr. Harkness. I'll be so glad to have you for a friend. And won't you please call me Robin? You see everyone who's ever liked me real well called me that and it'll make me feel homey here."

"Well, just between *us*, Miss - Robin." And the old man went off with a mysterious smile that even Budge's sour face could not dispel.

The house was very still. Mr. Allendyce was in his room writing some letters. The early dinner had been over for sometime. Robin wondered what Beryl was doing now and where she was - probably upstairs somewhere.

"I'll go and find her!"

This was more easily said than done for Gray Manor had wiggly wings and corridors turning in every direction and little stairs here and there so that one first went up and then down and then up again. Robin had almost given up her search and had just about decided she was lost, for turn whichever way she might, nothing seemed familiar, when she heard the harsh, scraping strains of a violin, vibrant with stormy feeling.

"I'll find that and then maybe it'll be someone who can tell me how to get back to the library," she thought, laughing silently at the ridiculousness of being lost in a house, anyway.

She traced the music to a turning which led into a narrow hallway. At its end a door stood ajar and from it a light streamed. Robin approached the door on tip toe that she might not disturb the music, then stood still on its threshold in delighted amazement for the violin player was the girl for whom she was seeking.

At sight of Robin the girl flung the violin upon the bed.

"Oh, please don't stop. May I come in? I was hunting for you."

It was an absurdly small room as compared to the great rooms below, and very bare. There was one chair which Beryl, scowling, pushed forward, at the same time sitting upon the bed. Her eyes said plainly: "What do you want?"

Robin ignored her unfriendliness. She sat down on the edge of the bed, close to Beryl.

"I'm awfully glad I found you," she ventured. "You see you're the only other *young* person in this house. Though I never had any chums like most girls do, Jimmie always seemed young and the birds and the flowers and the Farri children made it -" Robin stopped suddenly, for Beryl was staring at her with rude amusement. "I - I thought it would be so nice if you - and I - could be - sort of chums," she managed to finish.

Beryl tossed her head as she moved away, shutting the violin in its case with an angry little slam.

"I guess it *would* be sort of," she mocked.

"What do you mean?" Poor Robin's heart beat furiously; it had taken all the courage she could muster to force her advance upon this girl and Beryl's rebuff hurt her deeply. She flushed at Beryl's scornful laugh.

"Why - we're as far apart as the poles," Beryl answered. "You're - Gordon Forsyth. And I'm just Beryl Lynch."

Robin's eyes were like a baby's in their lack of understanding.

"I don't see -" she began but Beryl would not let her go on. Beryl's whole soul went out in resentment at what she suspected was "patronizing." "Not me!" she cried in her heart. And aloud: "Oh, you just *say* you can't see. Why I'm like a servant here. Though I won't be that way long with that old crank as uncivil as she is. Mother didn't want me to do it. But I wanted the money. And I'm going to stick it out, much as I hate it -"

Robin watched the other girl's stormy face in an ecstasy of delight. Here was a creature different from anyone she had ever known; almost her own age, too, full of the fire and spirit and daring which she longed to possess and knew she did not;

beautifully straight and tall.

"I asked old Budge for the place. I heard she wanted someone to help her and it was work anyone could do. Mother felt dreadfully - she said I'd hate it. I don't mind the work but I hate - oh, feeling I'm not as good as anyone here. When Mrs. Budge told me to put on a clean uniform - ugh, how I hate those uniforms - and go down to the hall to meet you, I told her I wouldn't. She 'most sent me off then and there."

"You did go, though. I saw you," Robin broke in.

"Oh, yes, I went but I wouldn't change my dress just to spite her. And I was curious to see the boy they were all making such a fuss about. You just ought to know how upset they were when *you* came! Why, old Budge talked as though it were a disgrace for a Forsyth to be a girl. I was glad - because it fooled her." Beryl realized suddenly that she was growing friendily confidential. She sharpened her tone. "*You'd* better go down before the old snoop catches you here."

"I wish you wouldn't talk like that," pleaded Robin.

"Like what?"

"Oh, as though we weren't - well just girls alike and couldn't be friends. We might have such good times -"

"You *are* a funny little kid, aren't you? And you certainly don't know how things are run in stiff houses like this. If old Budge could hear you! I don't mind telling you that the old cat keeps saying she's going to watch you to see if you act like a Forsyth. So you'd better not let her hear you asking to be friends with me."

Robin slowly rose to her feet, two bright spots of color flaming in her cheeks.

"Why, I'll -" Her anger died suddenly and a quaint little

dignity fell upon her. She straightened her slender figure and held her head very high. "I am a Forsyth and I shall act just as I think a good Forsyth should and not as Mrs. Budge thinks. And please don't think I'm the least bit afraid of this Mrs. Budge."

Beryl laughed so gleefully at Robin's defiance that Robin joined in with her and the friendship for which she sought sprang into being - all because of an unspoken alliance against the hostile housekeeper.

"I'll go back now - if you'll show me the way."

"They *ought* to have signs at every turning."

"Oh, what a funny thought!" And giggling, the two tiptoed through the winding corridors and down the stairs which led to the second floor.

"I'll see you tomorrow," whispered Robin at parting.

"It won't do - you'll see it won't do!" warned Beryl. "I haven't been in this house two whole days without knowing what it's like!"

CHAPTER VIII

ROBIN ASSERTS HERSELF

The coming of Percival Tubbs to Gray Manor added the one sweet drop to poor Mrs. Budge's cup of bitterness. Though he brought vividly back heartbreaking memories of young Chistopher the Third's school days, when she had waited each day for the lad's boisterous charge upon the kitchen after the "bite" which was his and her little secret, she hoped to find in him an ally. *He* would see how ridiculous it was to have a Forsyth girl, anyway, and especially a girl who limped around the house like a scared rabbit, afraid to ask for a crumb. If this Gordon had been a boy, as they had planned, another comely, happy youth, why, she could have soon learned to love him. But a girl - how would she look sitting at Master Christopher's desk, in his chair! Something was all wrong somewhere, but Percival Tubbs would find out and say what's what.

With this hope strong in her breast she made excuse to go into the Chinese room, for the Chinese room was only separated from the library by heavy curtains through which voices could be easily overheard. And Harkness had said the lawyer and the tutor were talking in the library.

Robin's guardian had given much thought to this interview with the tutor. Robin's fate worried him not a little. He had, in the few days, grown very fond of Robin, and he hated to leave her with Harkness and Budge and this Percival Tubbs, a poor sort of companionship where a fifteen-year-old girl's

Jane Abbott

happiness was concerned.

"I must make Tubbs see that the child is different -" he was thinking just as Mrs. Budge tiptoed into the Chinese room.

"Miss Gordon is not like other children and you'll have to plan your school work a little differently with her," he began, speaking slowly. "She's bright enough and knows much more about some things than most girls her age - and nothing at all about others. What I want you to do is to go easy; easy, that's it. I rather imagine she's always taken a lot on her own shoulders and I don't believe she's ever thought much of herself. If you can develop a little assertiveness in her - she'll need it, here -"

"Yes. She'll need it here," echoed the tutor, because he thought he ought to say something. He was a tall, lanky man whose shoulders sagged as though something about them had broken under the strain of being dignified; his face narrowed from an impressive dome of a forehead to a straggling Van Dyke beard which he always stroked with the fingers of his left hand. He was the old type of schoolmaster whom the rapid forward stride of education had left far behind. His summons to Gray Manor had come rather in the way of a life-saver and he did not intend to allow the fact that the Forsyth heir had turned out to be a girl, perturb him in the least. And so long as his rooms at the Manor were comfortable, his food good and his salary certain, he could adapt himself to any fool theory this lawyer guardian might care to advance.

Mr. Allendyce stared hard at the other, his face wrinkled in his effort to say the right thing.

"Oh, let her have her head," he finished finally. And he liked that idea so well that he repeated it. "Let her have her head. Do you understand me? Never mind what's in the old school-books. If she'd rather take a walk than study Latin verbs, well, let her. I want her to be happy here - happy, that's most important. You've heard of flowers that bloom only in shelter and sunshine? This youngster isn't unlike -"

"Well, I never! No, I *never!... I never!*" Mrs. Budge's gasp, rising in a crescendo, almost betrayed her presence. She gave a pillow a mighty jab. As though it were not bad enough to bring the girl to the house in the first place without paying a man a fancy price to teach her to have her own way! "Flowers! Humph! Old fools -" Unable to endure another word in silence she stalked off to her own quarters.

In the butler's pantry she found Beryl arranging real flowers in a squatty Bristol glass bowl and humming gaily as she did so. Now Beryl should have beep upstairs marking the new linen and she should not be singing as though she owned the whole world. These two transgressions and the sight of the bright blossoms in the girl's hand brought the climax to the old woman's wrath. All Beryl's shortcomings tumbled off her tongue in an incoherent flow of ill-temper. A stormy scene resulted which left the old housekeeper spent and Beryl blazing with indignation.

Consequently, when poor Robin, depressed from her first hour with the tutor, trying not to feel that Gray Manor was going to be a prison instead of a castle, sought out her new friend she found her throwing her few possessions into a cheap suitcase that lay, opened, across her narrow bed.

"Oh, what are you doing?" cried Robin in alarm.

"I'm going - that's what. She fired me."

Robin's first thought upon awaking that morning had been of Beryl; she had suffered the keenest impatience all through the trying morning, longing to go in search of her new friend. She could not lose her now - for a hundred Budges.

"Oh, I won't let you go!"

"A lot *you* could do!" cried Beryl scornfully, tears very close. "I

Jane Abbott

just can't please the old thing. But I hate to go home." She sat down, dolefully, on the edge of the bed. "I wanted to stay until I had earned two hundred dollars."

Two hundred dollars! That seemed such a very big amount of money to Robin that she sat silent, thinking about it.

Beryl, misinterpreting her quiet, tossed her head. "I s'pose that doesn't mean much to you. But it does to me - 'specially when I have to earn it." Then, with a flash of temper: "What do you know about wanting some one thing with all your whole heart and knowing just where you can get it and not having the money?"

Beryl made her tragedy very real and pouring out her troubles always brought her a grain of comfort.

"I've never had a thing in my life that I wanted," she finished.

"Oh, Beryl, I'm so sorry."

"Sorry! Why, a lucky little thing like you are can't even know what I'm talking about. That's why I said we couldn't be friends. *I've* had to work at home like a slave ever since I can remember. Pop's sick all the time and cross, and poor mother looks so tired and tries to be so cheerful and brave that your heart aches for her. And even when you're poor, a girl wants things, pretty things and to do things like other girls - and work as hard as you can you can't ever seem to reach them. I get just sick of it. I thought - if I could get this money -"

"Did you want it for your mother?" broke in Robin, sympathetically.

Beryl's face flushed redder. "Well, not exactly. That's the way it always is in books, but in life, when you're poor, it's each fellow for himself and there's not any time for your grand sounding self-sacrifice. I wanted it to buy a violin. That thing I've got's nothing but a cheap old fiddle. And I can play - I *know* I can play, or could if I could get a good violin. I took lessons from an old Belgian who lived above us and I played once for Martini at the theatre and he said - but what's the use of caring? What's the use of *thinking* about it? All a girl like me can do is just want big things!"

"Oh, Beryl," breathed Robin, a tremble on her lips. She wanted very much to make Beryl understand that she was not the "lucky thing" Beryl thought her; that she knew, too, what it was to want something and not to have it, though perhaps she had not known it as cruelly as Beryl had, for Jimmie had always contrived to cover their bleak moments with a makeshift contentment. "Oh, Beryl, honestly I know just how you feel. I wish I could help you. Maybe I can. My allowance seems awfully big and I can't ever spend it all -"

"Well, I'm not a beggar and I'm not hinting for your money," flared Beryl.

"I didn't mean -" Robin began, then faltered. Beryl had spoken with such real anger that she was frightened. Beryl, turning back to her packing, gathered up an armful of clothing on top of which lay an oblong bundle. Its wrappings were old and loose so that as Beryl flounced her burden toward the suitcase, the content of the package slipped out and down to the floor. Robin stared in amazement for there lay a doll in faded satin finery.

With a short, ashamed laugh, Beryl picked it up. "*that* old thing," she exclaimed, in half-apology.

Robin caught her arm. "Wait - oh, wait - let me see it!"

"It's just an old doll I've kept."

"It - it looks like my Cynthia. Oh, *please* just let me look at it. It's like a doll - I lost, once, ever so long ago." She examined the pretty clothing.

Now Beryl stared at Robin as though to find in her face a likeness to the little girl who had deserted her doll.

"Lost? And I found it in Sheridan Square. A little girl went off and left it. I waited awhile, then I took the doll home."

"Oh, how funny! How *funny*! It was me, Beryl. I'd been playing and Mr. Tony called to me to hurry and I forgot - and you found it. Why, I cried myself to sleep night after night thinking poor Cynthia was unhappy somewhere."

"And I called her my orphan doll and loved her because I thought she missed her real mother -"

"She was the loveliest dolly I ever had!"

"She was the loveliest dolly I ever saw!"

Both girls burst into a peal of laughter. They sat on the edge of the bed, the doll between them, the packing forgotten.

Robin clapped her hands. "And to think we find each other now. It's like a story. I went back to the park all alone that evening and would have been lost if it hadn't been for my -" she broke off short and flushed. She was going to tell Beryl about her play-prince but then, Beryl might laugh and she did not want that.

Beryl's face suddenly grew grave as she smoothed out a fold of the doll-garment.

"I always kept the doll put away. I never played with it because -" She hesitated a moment. "That night that I found the doll was a dreadful night. I wasn't quite six but I'll always remember it. At first mother and I were so happy, over finding the doll and because Pop had just gotten a raise. It seemed as though everything were going to be wonderful and we felt as rich as could be. We called the doll a lucky doll. And mother dressed me up in her green beads that Father Murphy, back in

Ireland, had given her when she told him she was going to marry Pop. And we had dumplings - ugh, I've hated dumplings ever since. And then -"

"What happened?"

"They came for Mom, some man from the hospital. Pop had been terribly hurt. And, well - nothing's been lucky since. It's just as I said; mother's had to work and Dale's had to work and Pop just sits in a chair and scolds and - well, I never wanted to take the doll out when mother could see it - after all that."

Robin made no effort to conceal how deeply Beryl's story had moved her. "Oh, Beryl, I'm so sorry. But maybe things will change. They'll have to - Jimmie always said, it's a long lane that has no turning. I'm so glad it was you who found my Cynthia. It might have been some one who wouldn't have loved her at all."

"I s'pose you ought to have her now."

"Oh, no, no. She's yours. Anyway, that doesn't matter," and Robin added triumphantly, "because we're really truly friends now, no matter what you say. Cynthia has brought us together."

Beryl shook her head.

"That old crank -" she began.

Robin stamped her foot in impatience. "I don't care a bit about Mrs. Budge. My guardian told me that I could have anything I wanted here just for the asking and he's made me the silliest big allowance that three girls couldn't spend. Oh, I've a plan! Ought not a girl like me have a companion? Don't they most always in books? You shall stay here at Gray Manor as my - chum."

Beryl still looked doubtful. "I'm too young -"

"That's just why I want you. Oh, I just can't bear to think of my guardian going away and leaving me here alone. You see I promised myself that I'd be happy while Jimmie's having his chance - that's why I came, you know. But this house is so big and so old and Mr. Harkness and Mrs. Budge are so old that I know it's going to be hard not to think of Jimmie and our lovely home and the birds. But if you'd stay it would be easier. Oh, say you will, say you will."

Beryl stared at Robin with a suspicious scrutiny. She firmly believed that rich people never did anything except for themselves and Robin, no doubt, was like all the others. Yet she was such a queer little thing that perhaps she *was* trying to be "nice" to her and make a soft place for her. And Beryl would not allow *that* for a moment.

"You can study with me, too. That Mr. Tubbs isn't so very bad. And we'll read together out of all those books in the library. And play - I never ad a real chum because Jimmie thought the girls and boys who went to he school I did, might make fun of my being lame. Poor Jimmie, he lways minded my being lame much more than I did because he's an artist nd shivers when anything isn't perfect. You shall have a bed in my oom - there's ever so much space. Oh, say you will."

Beryl frowned, uncertainly. "I don't want a penny I don't earn. But if I can really *do* things for you -"

"Oh, of course you can, lots of things. But you shan't wear those niforms - for then you wouldn't be a girl like me. Oh, we'll have *such* un. Let's take this stuff right down."

It took the girls only a very little time to transfer Beryl's belongings and to establish them in Robin's room, Beryl working mechanically, unable to believe her good fortune. Then, at Robin's command, she followed her while she went in search of her guardian.

Cornelius Allendyce and Percival Tubbs, sitting in a blue cloud of cigar smoke, were pleasantly discussing the pros and cons of the tariff question upon which they agreed, when Robin interrupted them.

"Please excuse me, but this is very important." Her breathlessness startled the two men. "I've engaged Beryl to be my chum. I - I thought I might be lonely here at Gray Manor. I want her to study with me, too. And do everything. This is she."

Cornelius Allendyce's mouth had dropped open from sheer amazement; suddenly it broadened into a grin. Here was Miss Gordon taking her "head" at once, without so much as one lesson. He glanced at Percival Tubbs but that good gentleman was stroking his silky beard quite indifferently.

"I'd rather have Beryl than anyone else, 'cause she's almost my own age and we like each other. Shall I tell Mrs. Budge or -"

"Without so much as a by-your-leave!" murmured the guardian. He surveyed Beryl; she seemed like a wholesome, spirited sort and the idea of a little companion for Miss Gordon was not a bad one, not at all - strange he hadn't thought of it.

"Perhaps, Miss Gordon, you'd better tell her yourself. You must begin - holding your own, my dear. Don't forget - ever, that you are a Forsyth, and that name has great power over Hannah Budge."

Robin did not stop to ponder what he meant or why a twinkle shone in his eyes. She rang the bell as her guardian indicated, then waited with a resolute squaring of her small chin, for Harkness' coming.

"Please, Mr. Harkness, will you bring Mrs. Budge here? There's something I want to tell you both."

Mrs. Budge, as she hunted out a clean apron, grumbled at the unusual summons.

"The girl herself, you say?" she asked, as she followed Harkness to the library.

Her astonishment changed to white wrath when Robin, standing by her guardian's chair, spoke.

"I wanted to tell you that Beryl Lynch is going to stay here as my companion. I'm going to give her half of my room so that I won't be lonely and please set a place for her next to me at the table."

Once again Cornelius Allendyce caught the twinkle in the butler's eye which should not be in a Forsyth butler's eye at all. But there was no twinkle about Mrs. Budge; her cheeks puffed in her effort to speak without strangling.

"If that piece -" she began, but she was quickly interrupted from every side. Both Harkness and Cornelius Allendyce cried out, the one pleadingly, the other in warning: "Careful, Mrs. Budge." Then Robin stepped forward and slipped her hand through Beryl's arm.

"Please, Mrs. Budge, I have made Beryl promise to stay. She didn't want to but I begged her. And if anyone is unkind to her it's just the same as being - unkind to me. That is all," she finished grandly, with an imperious little motion of her hand that waved the irate woman from the room before she knew she was moving.

"Now you can't say as that wasn't like a Forsyth," asserted Harkness, proudly, belowstairs. "If Missy wants a young lydy for a companion, well, she's a right to the kind of young lydy she wants." But Budge had escaped the reach of his voice.

In the library Cornelius Allendyce was patting Robin on the head.

"Well, you've won out in the first skirmish, my dear. But keep your weapons at hand."

Jane Abbott

CHAPTER IX

THE LYNCHS

The only thing that made the Lynch's cottage any different from the two hundred others at the mills, was that it stood at the end of a dreary row and therefore had a window on the side of its living room which overlooked the hills and the river.

This window was Moira Lynch's delight. Her poor, big Danny could sit in it all day long. And from it she herself could watch the setting sun flame over the crest of the hills and the narrow river shake off its workaday dress and go racing into the shadows of the woods. Poor Moira, years of heartbreaking work and worry had not changed her very much from the girl who had liked to lie in the deep sweet grass of her dear Ireland and let her fancy follow the winging birds into a land of dreams.

The other window of the tiny living room looked out directly upon the muddy road, across to the freight tracks.

It was to this window that Moira Lynch ran now, peering as far up the road as she could see.

"Beryl's late today," she said, with an anxious note.

"Well, what if she is? Things don't run by the clock," Danny Lynch answered testily. "You're always fussing. If it isn't the girl it's over Dale."

Mrs. Moira ignored the edge of crossness in her Danny's voice. She went to him, smoothed the spotless cushion at his back and put a fresh magazine on his table.

"It's a silly, worryin' hen I am," she laughed. (But, oh, her laugh was a tragic thing, for while her lips curved in a smile her eyes shadowed at their mockery).

"But things seem a bit different, today," she added, apologetically.

And just as Danny Lynch's retort of derision died away Beryl burst upon them.

Her mother needed only to give her one look to know that something *was* different.

"And what is it, my darlin'? It's that hungry I was getting to set my eyes on you. Two hours late you are, Beryl."

Beryl welcomed this reproach as it gave her an opportunity to impart her good news in an impressive way.

"I couldn't get away a minute sooner. I've a new position." She was going to say "job" but it did not seem fitting.

"What? Without so much as a word to your father and mother? And did the likes of that old housekeeper fire you?"

Beryl had no intention of telling of her ignominious fray with Mrs. Budge.

"I'm engaged to be a companion to Gordon Forsyth!" she answered, grandly.

At this Moira Lynch dropped a spoon with a loud clatter.

"A companion to - that new boy who's come to the Manor?"

Beryl, recognizing that her story needed detailed explanation, slipped off her outer wraps, threw them into a chair, kissed her father lightly on his cheek, perched herself on the old sofa and proceeded to tell the story of Gordon Forsyth's coming to Gray Manor while her mother listened with breathless interest.

"And it's a girl she is - a little lame girl!"

"The queerest kid you ever saw. Not a bit snippy or rich acting. She doesn't get at all excited over her new clothes and bossing those old fogeys around and ordering her motor any minute she wants it. She thinks the little place she lived in in New York is lots nicer than Gray Manor. When you look at her you think she's a baby and then when she talks, why - she seems older than I am! But she's funny like you, Mom; she's always pretending things are different from what they are and giving them names. She calls old Budge the wicked woman who wanted to eat the two children," Beryl giggled. "And she calls the Mills a Giant."

Moira Lynch's face beamed with joyous understanding. Here was a fellow-soul, "funny" like herself, Beryl described her; Beryl, for whom black was always and invariably black, and a spade a spade.

"Why, she even wanted to come down here with me," Beryl finished.

There were so many questions trembling on Moira's tongue that, for the moment, supper was neglected. Not long, however; the striking of the clock reminded her that in a very few minutes Dale would be home, hungry. Her mission in life, next to tending her big Danny, was feeding her two children. For tonight she had made Beryl's favorite dessert, a bread pudding, the eggs for which she had carefully hoarded during several days' denial. Beryl, keeping up a running fire of talk, spread the cloth on the centre table and brought the dishes from the cupboard.

"By'n by, you'll be too fine for the rest of us," broke in big Danny upon their chatter, the usual discordant tone in his voice.

"Well, I guess it won't be your fault if I am," Beryl flared. "Everything that I've gotten I've gotten for myself and I don't know of anyone ever trying to help me."

Like a flash the little mother was between the two, a soothing hand on the father's shoulder.

"Now don't you two be a-spoiling this night," she laughed a bit hysterically. "Of course our girl's going to be too fine for anyone, but it's always a-loving she'll be to her Dad and her Mommy." She declared it with an ardent triumph. This mother who had once dreamed things for herself dreamed them now for her boy and girl. From Beryl's infancy she had taught her to want "fine things." And Beryl wanted them with all her heart and, with youth's selfishness, wanted them for herself, alone.

After her father's taunt, Beryl, with sullen resentment, locked her lips on her other pleasant experiences. Nor would she tell now how Robin had written to her guardian to send down a real violin for her to practice upon, or what fun it was to study with Mr. Percival Tubbs, whose ears were distractingly like Brussels sprouts. And that she learned much, much faster than Robin did! Poor Robin was always wondering the why of everything.

Her mother suddenly exclaimed: "It's Father Murphy's beads you shall wear this night, my girl. Didn't the good soul, God rest him, give them with his blessing? Watch the potatoes while I get them."

Moira's beads had always played a significant part in her life. They marked what she called her "blessings." Without doubt the rare bright spots in her life shone like blessings for the dark of their background. Years ago, when her Danny had had his accident and her world had seemed to turn upside down until it rested, full-weight, upon her poor shoulders, her "blessing" had been Miss Lewis at the settlement. Miss Lewis had given her work so that she could earn money to feed her family; Miss Lewis had sent the chair to Danny; Miss Lewis had found cheaper lodgings and had helped her make them homelike. Another blessing had been Jacques Henri, the old Belgian who lived above them and whose violin had attracted Beryl as the magnet draws the iron. A lonely soul, he had found sweet company in the child and had gladly helped the eager fingers. Later he had come down to supper with them and Beryl had played a "piece" for her Pop, wearing the beads in honor of the occasion. When Beryl had graduated from the graded school she had stood as class prophet before an assemblage of fond relatives, among them Dale and herself - wearing the green beads. Moira had wished Father Murphy were there to see her girl.

She clasped them around the girl's neck now with fingers that trembled and eyes bright with the tears which were always close to them. During the little ceremony Dale burst in like a gust of strong, sweet air.

"Hullo, everybody! M'm'm, something smells good! What's for tonight, Mom? Salt pork and thick gravy? Fried potatoes? Good! Hullo, Sis. How goes it, Pop?" His greeting embraced everything and everyone in a rush, from the savory supper to the invalid father whose face had brightened at his coming.

"What're you getting all dolled up for, Sis?"

Beryl and her mother tried to tell the story at the same time. Dale did not seem at all impressed and Beryl was disappointed. He said he had heard in the mills that the newcomer at the Manor was a girl, and lame, too. He didn't know what difference it made to any of them, anyway. He scowled a little as he said it.

Dale had his father's strong body and his mother's face of a dreamer; his eyes were brooding like Beryl's but his mouth was wide and tender and might have seemed weak but for the strength in the square cut jaw.

Since that time, ten years back, when he had resolutely put behind him his precious ambitions and had taken the first job he could find, he had been the recognized head of the family. As such he turned to Beryl now.

"I suppose you'll let this rich little girl wipe her feet on you and you'll love it," he said with such scorn that Beryl turned hot and cold in speechless anger.

"Now, sonny, now, sonny. Let's wait until we know the poor little thing," begged his mother.

But for Beryl, except for the fun of wearing the beads, all joy for the moment had fled. She had particularly wanted to impress Dale with her good fortune. She had often, of course, heard Dale speak scathingly and bitterly of the "classes" and the "privileged few" and the unfairness of things in general, but she had paid little attention to it and could not, anyway, connect it with unassuming Robin. When he met Robin, he'd understand - and while Dale ate ravenously and talked to his father between mouthfuls, she planned how she would bring Robin to supper the very next time she came home, despite her vow that she would never let Robin see how humble and small her home was.

After supper Beryl helped her mother clear away and Dale brought out his "plaything" which was what he laughingly called the contrivance of strings and spools and little wooden wheels he had made and which he and his father "played with" each evening. Beryl had often wondered why Dale seemed to care so much about it; why he spent hours and hours drawing and figuring on bits of paper. Of course it amused the father, who, during the day, cut the spools into tiny wheels, with a sharp jack-knife; but it must be stupid for Dale to spend all of his evenings over the silly thing. Beryl often lounged on the back of his chair and listened to discover whether there was any part of the game she might like.

Tonight Dale's interest seemed forced.

"If I could just find out what's needed *here* -" he growled, touching the delicate contrivance. "That's the way! While I'm racking my poor old nut, some other fellow's going to make the whole thing out!"

Danny Lynch's big hand trembled where it lay on the table. "If I had had the learning -" he began. "I could help, mebbe."

Dale hastened to comfort him. "You don't get that stuff from books, exactly, Pop. It comes here," touching his head. "If I only had the money to have the thing made in metal. Oh, well, what's the use of talking. The thing's got my goat, though. I'm thinking about it all the time. Say, Mom, can I bring Adam Kraus over to supper some night? He said he'd like to meet Pop and he's a good sort."

This Adam Kraus had only recently come to the Mills. He had at first impressed the neighborhood somewhat unfavorably, for he encouraged a suggestion of mystery, lived at the Inn, kept aloof from everyone, and seemed to have no family. Moira's own quick thought of him when Dale had pointed him out on the road in front of the Mill store was that "he looked too white for a working man." But he seemed to have singled Dale out for his advances; Dale thought he was a good sort and had met him more than half-way; Dale who had had to work too hard by day and study at night to make any close friendships. Whether she liked him or not, he should have the best she could offer.

"*I'm* going to bring Robin - I mean, Miss Forsyth, down here the next time *I* come," broke in Beryl.

"And of course you can. And Dale shall bring his friend, too."

"And you can wear your fine beads, Sis," finished Dale, teasingly.

"And it's a nice pot roast and cabbage salad we'll have, too. And a bit of the fruit cake with real butter sauce." Wasn't she going to get her check soon from the store to which she sent her lace?

So Beryl forgot her vexation and Dale his problem with his wooden toy in pleasant anticipation of the "dinner party," as Mrs. Moira grandly called it, out of respect to the pot roast and the fruit cake which Miss Lewis had sent them and which was hidden away in a huge crock in the shed.

"Mom, can't I take the beads back with me? They're so pretty and I haven't a thing that's nice," begged Beryl as the moment for her to return to the Manor came.

"The Princess and the Beggar-maid!" laughed Dale.

"My fine lady must have her jewels!" added big Danny.

Beryl flushed under their teasing but held her tongue, for didn't she always have that picture blazed in her heart of the moment when with her violin she would hold enthralled her unappreciative family and thousands of others? *Then* they would not laugh at her!

"I'll be ever so careful of them and only wear them once in a while," she promised.

Though Mrs. Moira would, of course, have given her children anything they wanted that was hers, she hesitated now, not from reluctance to part with her one "pretty" but because suddenly out of the silent past came the old father's words: "They are only beads. But they'll remind you of this day." She had been seventeen then - a slip of a girl. Beryl was almost sixteen now.

"The shame to me! Sure, it's only beads they are!" she laughed, with a little catch in her voice. "Of course you shall take them."

CHAPTER X

THE LADY OF THE RUSHING WATERS

"What'll we do today?"

Beryl asked the question, turning from her post between the curtains of Robin's sitting-room. Not in a tone of complaint did she speak, rather as though weighing which pastime would be most worthy of the unexpected holiday.

For poor Percival Tubbs had "neuralgy" and could not leave his room; Harkness had told them when he carried in their breakfast.

"*This* is just the kind of a day you'd like *something* to happen," Beryl went on, permitting a sigh to convey how much she would welcome that something. "It's all gray and mysterious. The hills look awfully far away. It's lonesomey."

Robin looked anxiously to her companion. *She* did not feel lonesome at all. This room, where they ate their breakfast each morning at Harkness' suggestion, was cosy and full of inviting books and pretty pictures and comfy chairs; Harkness was ever so nice and concerned as to their comfort, they were as secure from Mrs. Budge's hostility as thick walls and Harkness' vigilance could make them and - best of all, a letter from her Jimmie, full of Mr. Tony's plans and their contemplated sailing, lay close to her heart.

Jane Abbott

"What would you like most to do, Beryl?"

"Oh, let's ask Williams to take us for a long ride - I adore going like the wind," answered Beryl promptly.

This suggestion appealed to Robin, who, although she didn't like to "go like the wind," never tired of riding among the hills. She went immediately with Beryl to find Williams, the chauffeur. Williams, like the others around the Manor, with the exception of Mrs. Budge, had fallen under Robin's spell and was enjoying the stir that her coming brought to the old house. So he declared, now, that it would be a "nice day for a run" and they could take the Cornwall road, because there was a fellow in Cornwall he ought to see.

Before the holiday fun could begin Beryl had her "duties" to perform. These were tasks which she had set for herself so that she might not feel for one moment that she was living on Robin's charity and were most of them quite unnecessary and little things that Robin would really like to do herself. However Beryl was too proudly intent upon saving her pride to realize this and Robin, instinctively understanding, let her have her way.

Finally started, the girls snuggled close together in the car, holding hands under the big robe. And, as they sped over the smooth road, each let her thoughts take wings. Beryl's, with the honest self-centredness that was characteristic of her, fluttered about herself. How she looked in this peachy car - how she'd love to steer it and just step on the gas and fly; some day, when she was famous, she'd have a car like this only much bigger and painted yellow and she'd take Mom and Pop out and go through the Mill neighborhood so that that gossipy Mrs. Whaley who had called her "stuck-up" could see her. What she'd do in Robin's shoes, anyway! Why, Robin didn't know what money meant, probably because Robin had never wanted any one big thing, like she did.

Robin, beside her, sat in cosy contentment - mainly because of her precious letter. She drew a mental picture of her Jimmie, sailing away. Then her thoughts came back to the gray hills and she wished her father might see them at that moment, so as to paint them. He would love Wassumsic, she knew - but, oh, he would hate the Mills. He would think, as she did, that it was too bad they had built the Mill cottages between the dingy buildings and the freight yards when they might have built them where each window could have overlooked the climbing fields and woods, where the children could have played in sweet grass the livelong day and built beautiful snow forts when it was winter.

Beryl suddenly broke the silence by a gleeful "Isn't this fun?" as Williams coasted down a long grade with a breath-catching acceleration of speed.

The wind had whipped a fine color into the girls' cheeks, the changing scenes about them were of untiring interest; they exclaimed delightedly over each curve and hill in the road, each tiny hamlet through which they passed. All too soon, they reached Cornwall and started on the homeward way.

At the top of a steep hill Williams slowed down to slip the gear into second. In the valley below them was a collection of unpainted houses, leaning towards one another as though for protection against the growing things about them.

"The Forgotten Village!" cried Robin. "Don't you feel just as though we might tumble over into it?"

"A good place to drive right *through*," Williams answered with a scornful laugh.

Alas, poor Williams - he brought the car skilfully and safely down the difficult hill only to have it stop, with a reproachful snort, in the very heart of the little village.

"What's the matter?" asked the girls in one breath as Williams, with an explosive exclamation, jumped from his seat.

There was a moment of investigation, before the man replied.

"No gas!".

"Is *that* all?"

"All! I'll say that's enough - here. Don't look as though anyone'd know what gas is in these parts. You sit in the car while I ask someone, Miss Forsyth."

"You wanted something to happen, Beryl," laughed Robin, as Williams walked away.

"Pooh! *This* isn't much of an adventure. And I'm awfully hungry."

Poor Williams returned with the word that he'd have to walk on to the next town - unless he was lucky enough to meet someone who'd help him out. He advised the girls waiting in the store.

"There isn't even a telephone in this dump," he grumbled resentfully, quite forgetting that he had only his own care-lessness to blame for the whole thing.

Neither Robin nor Beryl had the slightest intention of waiting in the funny little store where the crackers and tea and coffee looked as old as the old man who came out from behind the counter at their approach. They waited until Williams had disappeared, then went forth to explore the Forgotten Village. Unabashed, they stared at the weather-beaten houses, at the old woman, a faded shawl tied around her head, washing clothes at a pump, at the hideous square of dingy brick which served as school house and church, its window frames stuffed here and there with rags, a pathetic sign upon which was printed "library," hanging crazily by one nail.

Beyond the church stood an old mill, its roof tumbled in. Exploring it the girls heard the sound of tumbling water and discovered a stream breaking its way through thick under-growth. A lane, marked by two wagon ruts, edged the course of the stream.

"Let's see where this goes," suggested Beryl.

Robin limped willingly after her. It was an alluring lane, even in November, for the ghostly gray branches of old trees met and interlocked close overhead, fir trees, mingling with the silver white trunks of slender birches, walled it either side, a whirring of invisible wings added to its apartness and the little stream, tumbling its way, sounded like laughter.

"Isn't this the loveliest spot? Wherever do you suppose it comes out?" For the lane twisted and turned as it climbed.

"Robin, there's a house!"

Ahead of them the girls could see through the trees the outlines of a low square house. And as they drew nearer, walking stealthily, they stared in amazement. For, unlike its neighbors in the village below, this house was as white as fresh white paint could make it, at the windows hung crisply white curtains, a brass knocker dignified its broad door.

Robin, always imaginative, clutched Beryl's arm with a breath-less giggle. "Beryl, it's like the house of bread and cake with the window panes of sugar. Do you suppose someone will call out: 'Tip-tap, tip-tap, who raps on my door'?"

"Sh-h! I'm hungry enough to eat the roof. Let's ask for a drink of water so's to see the inside."

Robin did not think it was just nice to deliberately intrude upon the privacy of this shut-away house but Beryl, not waiting for her approval, knocked boldly on the heavy old door.

When the door swung open, however, and a beaked-nosed

Jane Abbott

woman, absurdly like the witch of the fairy story, confronted the girls, Beryl stood tongue-tied and Robin had to come to the rescue.

"Can we - if you please, we had an accident - I mean, we went for a walk - oh, *may* we have a drink of water?" she floundered, fairly blinking before the sharply piercing eyes of the woman in the door.

"Who is it, Brina?" came from within, whereupon the woman answered in rapid German, her head turned backward over her shoulder, her hand still on the doorknob.

"Shame on you, Brina. They are two children - lost, perhaps. Let them come in."

The room was disappointingly like any other old country-house living room; scrupulously clean and shining, a wide fireplace aglow with a wood fire that cast bright splotches of color over the low walls, the faded rag rugs, the piece-work cushions on the old wooden settle.

Close to its warmth sat a white-haired woman, one long thin hand supporting her head in such a way as to keep her face in a shadow.

Robin explained their presence in the lane, incoherently, for there was something frightening about the silent, composed figure and the intentness with which those shadowed eyes scrutinized her. While Robin talked, Beryl swiftly surveyed the room and its occupants, not least of which was a great St. Bernard dog, that, after one "gr'f f" leaned against his mistress' chair and regarded the intruders with watchful eyes as though to reserve advances, friendly or hostile.

Her account finished, Robin smiled bravely back into the grave face, with that enchanting tenderness which had won Cornelius Allendyce and enticed him to strange deeds.

The smile worked its spell at least on the dog for he moved slowly over to her, lifted a big paw and placed it gravely upon her shoulder.

"Caesar declares you a friend," said the woman in a slow, low-pitched voice. "He does not welcome many into our seclusion. Please sit down. Brina, bring these young ladies a pitcher of milk and some cookies."

Brina swung out of the room at her mistress' bidding. Robin, uncomfortable but immensely curious and excited, sat on the edge of the settle and chattered, while Beryl, well behind their silent hostess, made mysterious signs with fingers and lips and eyes.

"We think this is the loveliest spot - the old town and the mill and this lane - and all. No one would ever dream from the road that this house was here. Has it a name? First I called it the House of Bread and Cake and Sugar - like the fairy story, but it ought to be called the House of Rushing Waters, hadn't it?"

"That will do - very nicely. No, no one would know from the road that the house stands here."

But when Robin ventured: "Aren't you ever lonely?" there was a perceptible tightening of the lips that made her sorry she had asked it.

"Robin, there's something funny about that whole place," declared Beryl, half-an-hour later as they went back down the lane. "I was doing some thinking while you were talking."

"She's a dear old lady, Beryl. I feel sorry for her."

"Oh, yes, dear enough. *I* thought she was stand-offish. But you don't think for a moment she belongs 'round here, in the same town with that old cheese down at the store?"

Robin admitted that everything about her House of Rushing Waters was very different from the Forgotten Village.

"Wasn't that Brina just like a witch with her parrot nose and sharp eyes?"

But Beryl had no patience just now with Robin's beloved fairy lore. Two little lines wrinkled her brow.

"There's something queer about that place or my name isn't Beryl Lynch. And I like to know what's what. Wouldn't it be fun to find out what it is? Whether she's hiding there on account of something or someone's keeping her a prisoner? Maybe -" Beryl lowered her voice, "maybe she's crazy."

"Oh, Beryl, she didn't act a bit crazy. Just very sad. She was nice. I thought the room was lovely, too - and the lunch and that darling dog." Robin had thoroughly enjoyed the simple hospitality and meant to defend it.

"Of course the room was nice," Beryl felt that she showed much patience with Robin's obtuseness, "but didn't you see anything *different* in that room? Books and magazines! Country people don't sit and read magazines and knit on rose wool in the middle of the afternoon! Robin, *that* woman's a lady! And you notice she didn't tell us who she was. And a woman with her talking some foreign jibberish."

"Beryl, you're wonderful to notice all these things. I'd never have noticed half of them."

Beryl tossed her head with pride. "Nothing much escapes *me*," she boasted. "And I think it was a good thing we didn't tell her just who *we* were. But let's not let a soul know about our finding this place until we unravel the mystery."

Robin hesitated. "She was so nice to us and it's really none of our business why she's there or who she is -" she argued so staunchly that Beryl put in hastily: "Well, let's just have it a secret because secrets are such fun." And to that Robin agreed gladly, for secrets *are* fun and are always a strengthening bond in true friendship.

"I won't tell a soul!" she promised.

They found Williams waiting for them at the store, worried at their disappearance and annoyed at the delay. He had walked many miles in payment for his carelessness.

As they rushed homeward, both girls thought of the house they had left and its lonely occupant.

"Wouldn't wonder a *bit* if she might be some royalty person hiding here from anarchists," whispered Beryl, with a burst of imagination, amazing for her, tinged by a novel she had recently read.

"Would we dare go again to see her?"

"Of course we're going. Even if you don't, I want to find out who she is and all about her."

"*I'd* just like to see her again and that darling dog. If she doesn't want to tell us who she is I don't want her to! It's more fun to pretend that her house is made of bread and cake and sugar."

"Pooh!" was Beryl's impatient answer.

And that evening, as though in defense of her suspicions she thrust a newspaper under Robin's nose with an expressive "There, read *that!*" at the same time pointing to an inconspicuous paragraph.

The paragraph told of the mysterious disappearance of its Dowager Queen from the little warring Balkan kingdom of Altruria.

"She could be in this country as well as not. I read a book once where a Duke hid for five years right in the heart of New York and then met his heir face to face on Broadway. Wouldn't it be fun if that old woman *was* this Dowager Queen?"

"But, Beryl, she talked English. Wouldn't she talk - some other language?"

Beryl was not to be discouraged. "Dowagers don't. They talk ever so many tongues. English as good as any. I'll bet anything you say. You just wait."

CHAPTER XI

POT ROAST AND CABBAGE SALAD

The following Wednesday had been set for Mrs. Lynch's dinner of "pot roast and cabbage salad."

"You'll think we're awfully poor, Robin, when you see that mean old cottage," Beryl complained as the girls were dressing for the dinner.

Robin, hesitating between a Madonna blue and a yellow dress, turned quickly at the tone in Beryl's voice.

"Oh, Beryl, what difference does your house make! I want to know your mother and your father and - Dale."

"Well, there's no use your dressing up - it'll just make everything else there look absurdly shabby."

Robin laid the garment she held down upon the bed. A puzzled look darkened the glow in her eyes. There were a great many times when she found it difficult to understand Beryl's changing moods. She herself was too indifferent to clothes to know that it was the two pretty gowns she had brought out from her wardrobe that had now sent Beryl into the dumps.

"I won't dress up, Beryl. I just thought your mother would like to have me - out of respect to her party. I didn't think you wouldn't like it. But if you think I'm going down there to stare around at the things in the house and pick to pieces the dishes and the food - you're wrong, Beryl. I think your mother must be a wonderful woman and I am just crazy to meet her and I know I'm going to love your father and I never talked to a boy in my whole life except in school when I had to! There!" Robin stopped for very lack of breath.

This unexpected show of spirit, so unlike Robin's usual gentleness, took Beryl back. Fond as she was of her mother she had never thought of her as exactly "wonderful" or of anyone wanting to know her, or her poor, crippled father, or Dale. She laughed a little shamefacedly.

"Oh, wear what you want to, Robin. I suppose I'm jealous because I haven't anything except that old gray thing that's just tottering with age. What a joke to call Dale a boy! Why, he's never been a boy, because he's worked so hard for everything."

"Well, I'm glad I'm going to meet him, anyway." Robin spoke with excitement. It did not matter at all what she wore - without a moment's hesitation she put away the blue and the yellow dress and brought forth the mouse colored jersey she had worn when she arrived at Gray Manor - she was going to meet Beryl's family. Robin, who had never had any family except "Jimmie," imagined beautiful things of family life, mostly colored by books she had read and pictures she had seen. Brothers were always big strong fellows who sometimes teased their younger sisters but were always ready with a helping hand; fathers - well, she knew about fathers, having had Jimmie, but Beryl's father must be very different because of his accident. It was "Mom" that she most wanted to know. She hoped Beryl's mother would kiss her. At the thought her heart gave a quick little beat.

When Percival Tubbs, to whom Harkness, uncertain as to the propriety of a Forsyth dining at one of the Mill cottages had appealed, had mildly endeavored to point out to Robin that this dinner-party was not exactly "fitting," Robin had simply not been able to understand and had answered so honestly:

"Why, just because I'm a Forsyth doesn't make me a bit better than those people who work in the Mills, does it?" That Mr. Tubbs had abandoned his point with a mental reservation not unlike Mrs. Budge's beloved: "Things *are* going to sixes and sevens."

And below stairs the loyal Harkness, putting off his own doubt, had met Mrs. Budge's scorn of the whole "goings-on" with a grand defense of his little mistress: "Some lydies in 'igh places distribute their bounty in baskets but if Miss Gordon sees fit to carry 'ers in her pretty little 'eart, I don't say it's for us to be a thinking it isn't the 'appier way," and Budge knew he was very much in earnest because he forgot his h's, a little trick of speech he had long ago overcome.

For a finishing touch to her despised "best" dress, Beryl brought forth her green beads. Robin exclaimed over them, taking them out of Beryl's hand to hold them to the light.

"Oh, they are lovely, Beryl, see the deep glow! They're like the sea. You ought to be proud of them."

"They're just some beads an old priest gave mother when she was a girl," Beryl explained, making her voice indifferent. She loved Robin's enthusiasm but half-suspected it might be "put on" in order to make up to her for the things she did not have. "They do look nice on this dress, though, don't they?" She laid them against her neck and stared with satisfaction at the reflection in the long mirror.

The Lynch cottage, in honor of the occasion, sparkled with orderliness. Mrs. Moira looked very gay in a pretty foulard she had made over from two of Miss Lewis' old dresses; her fluttering hands alone betrayed her nervousness and her fears that though the most tempting smells came from the stove her dinner might not be "just right" for little Miss Forsyth and for Dale's new friend, too.

However, when Robin came into the room with Beryl she

Jane Abbott

looked so appealingly small that Mrs. Lynch promptly forgot she was a Forsyth and that the dinner might not be good enough and put her arms around her and kissed her. And Robin with an impulsive movement snuggled closer to the warm embrace.

"Why, it's a mite of a thing you are," cried Mrs. Moira with the singing note in her voice that always came when she was deeply moved. "And hungry, I hope. Well, Dale will be here in a moment and then we'll dish up."

Then everything was just like Robin had hoped it would be. Beryl's mother called them "children" and let them help her with the finishing touches of the dinner. Beryl's father smiled at her and patted her hand. She did not see the little room with Beryl's eyes, its limited space into which so much had to be crowded, the cracked shade on the lamp, the dingy carpeting that held together through some kind miracle, she only thought it cosy and homey; she liked the queer old clock and the blue bowl filled with artificial jonquils and the crocheted "tidies" with dogs designed in intricate stitches.

"Here's Dale!" whispered Beryl. "I'm crazy to meet his friend. I'm going to sit next to him at the table, see if I don't."

In the excitement of Dale's arrival and of introducing the strange "Mr. Kraus" no one noticed Robin for a moment, or that she stared at Dale with round, puzzled eyes. Had she ever seen him before? When Beryl turned suddenly and said: "Dale, this is Gordon Forsyth," she hoped he would say: "Why, I know her." However, he merely mumbled "How do you do," stiffly, and turned away, to Beryl's indignation and Robin's vague disappointment.

The pot roast and the cabbage salad were as delicious as Mrs. Moira's loving pains could make them; Dale's friend talked mostly to big Danny and Mrs. Moira listened and Dale occasionally put in a word. Over her plate Robin watched first one and then another, her eyes invariably coming back to

Dale's face. Beryl, annoyed that no one noticed her and Robin and treated them "as though they were just children," ate ravenously, in dignified silence.

The talk centered about the Mills. Adam Kraus freely ridiculed the Forsyth methods. "They're miles behind the times," he declared and compared them glibly with other similar industries. "Old Norris belongs to the has-beens. Look at the machinery he uses - all right in its day, of course. But if a fellow went to him with some new kind of a loom, would he look at it? Not he! The old's good enough."

"Hear that, Pop?" put in Dale, exchanging a meaning glance with his father.

"And look at the way they house the mill hands here, putting a fellow like Dale with his cleanness and his brains and his possibilities, into a dump like this. They don't recognize the human element in industries of this sort or what it's worth to them. Why, there's no argument any more as to the increased efficiency from giving better living conditions - but I'll bet Norris hasn't heard of it."

"We haven't been here long enough to know -" Mrs. Lynch began gently but Dale interrupted her, his voice rough.

"It isn't Norris alone, Adam. You've got to go further up - it's the House of Forsyth. They're feudal lords - or like to think they are. Do you suppose it mattered much up there, when the little Castle girl had her arm crushed in that old wheel last month and died because her body wasn't nourished enough to stand under the amputation? A lot they cared - just one bit of machinery gone for a day - another -"

"*Dale -*" cried Mrs. Lynch, in distressed embarrassment, and suddenly everyone looked at Robin.

Robin had been listening to Adam Kraus and Dale with deep interest. It was not until Mrs. Lynch exclaimed and all eyes turned in her direction that she connected what they were saying with her own self. Under Dale's sudden scrutiny she flushed.

"I forgot you were here, little Miss Forsyth." But this was so far from an apology that Mrs. Lynch looked more distressed than before and Beryl glared at her brother.

"Oh, *please* don't mind me," begged Robin. *She* was glad Dale did not say he was sorry for what he had been saying; she wanted to know more. She wanted to tell them that *She* called the Mills a Giant and that she hated them and that Cornelius Allendyce had told her she should look for a Jack who could climb the Bean Stalk, only she was afraid of the stranger and a little of Dale, too. "Won't you tell me all about the - the Castle girl?"

"There isn't much to tell about her that's different from ninety-nine other cases. She was supporting a younger brother and sister. The brother's only twelve years old but he had to go to work - said he was sixteen. The kid sister helps the grandmother as much as she can."

"Do they live in one of these houses?"

"In the old village. They're cheaper, you see. The boy can't earn as much as Sarah Castle did and they had to move up the river."

"Could I go to see them - sometime?"

Mrs. Lynch answered for Dale. "Of course you can, dearie. And I'll go with you. It's from my own county they say the grandmother comes and likely she'll know some of the old people."

"Oh, will you?" Robin's eyes shone like two deep pools reflecting starlight. "I'd like to know *everyone* here in the village and what they do. Perhaps the - the other Forsyths wanted to really know the Mill people, too, only they - they've been so unhappy. But I'm different, you see - I'm a girl and so sort of - little."

"Bless the warm little heart of her - defending her own," thought Mrs. Lynch, and Dale, his face softening until it was boyish, smiled and said: "You *are* a little thing, aren't you?"

At his smile, a wave of memory rushed over Robin with such suddenness that a breathless "oh" escaped her parted lips. A dark night and lonely streets, a chill wind cutting her face, an iron fence enclosing a deserted triangle of dead grass and filthy papers - a kind voice telling her not to cry - of course, her Prince! She peeped almost fearfully at Dale who was joking with Beryl. *He* did not know - he had forgotten, of course. He had been a big boy, then, and he had not gone on playing the little game the way she had. How wonderful, how *very* wonderful, to find him. And Beryl's brother! She did not mind at all what he had said about the Forsyth's. If he said it, it must be true. She would find out.

Mrs. Lynch, beaming over her simple dinner, little knew that Destiny sat at her board, shaping, moulding, gathering and weaving the threads of life, golden and drab.

To Beryl's disgust, after the meal Dale brought forth his "toy." But Adam Kraus, instead of showing the boredom which Beryl expected, studied it with absorbed keenness, quickly grasping what Dale wanted to do.

"Have you ever shown this to Morris?" he asked Dale.

Dale shook his head. "No use to do it now - until I've worked the thing out to perfection. And I can't do that - without money."

Robin, wiping plates for Mrs. Lynch, caught Dale's words and Adam Kraus' answer.

"I wonder if Norris would see what an invention like that - if you can make it do what you say you can - would be worth to these mills. It would lift them out of the boneyard of antiquity and put them fifty years ahead of their competitors. Why, I'll bet Granger's would give you a cool twenty thousand for that just as it stands. It would serve Norris right, too."

Dale's face flushed with excitement. "Do you really think all that, Adam? Pop and I've gotten so down in the dumps trying to work the thing out that we've lost our sense of values."

"Inventors never have any," laughed Kraus, with a change in his voice. And he commenced hastily to talk of other things, to Dale's disappointment.

Robin pulled timidly at Dale's arm.

"Who's Grangers?"

"Grangers? Don't you know the big mills up at South Falls?"

"Would they - if they took - that - you'd go there -" She tried desperately to voice the fear that had shaped in her heart; Grangers taking this funny wooden thing that Mr. Kraus said was worth so much, and Dale going away from Wassumsic, and Dale's mother - and Beryl.

"You just bet I would," and Dale laughed. "But don't worry, we won't be going for a while."

Robin had so much to think about that night that she could not go to sleep. She did not want to go to sleep. Up to this day she had been just little Robin Forsyth, "Red-Robin," at Gray Manor to let Jimmie have his chance; happy, because Jimmie was having his chance and Beryl was with her and Beryl was unfailingly interesting.

Now she realized that a Forsyth couldn't be just "anything." A Forsyth ought to care about those awful Mills, that were in some sort of a "boneyard," and about the people who worked in them - especially poor Sarah Castle's brother and sister. And there were probably many other boys and girls. She'd ask Mrs. Lynch - or Dale.

Beryl stirred and Robin ventured to speak.

"Beryl, are you awake? If Mr. Norris bought that invention of your brother's, would it make things easier for - the Mill people?"

Beryl jerked herself up on her elbow.

"Red-Robin Forsyth, are you crazy? Fussing over that absurd toy of Dale's at this hour? Why should *you* care?" Beryl sank back into her pillows and stretched. "Didn't Mr. Kraus have the most glorious eyes?"

Robin answered with amazing positiveness. "No, I hated his eyes. They were not true eyes. But - I like Dale - lots." And just here, for the second time, she locked her lips on her precious secret for Dale must never know that she remembered him; all that belonged to her childhood. Beryl might laugh, too, as she often did at her "fancies," and call her "funny."

Thinking of Dale brought her thoughts back to the Mills so that while Beryl snuggled her sleepy head back into her pillow, she stared at the thin shaft of light that shone under the door and wished she was big instead of "a little bit of a thing" and very wise so that she would know what to do to show these people in Wassumsic that she - a Forsyth, *did* care.

CHAPTER XII

ROBIN WRITES A LETTER

Cornelius Allendyce had returned to New York from Gray Manor with his mind pleasantly at ease so far as Gordon Forsyth was concerned. His associates noticed a certain smugness and satisfaction about him and they often caught him smiling at inappropriate moments and then pulling himself together as though his thoughts had been wandering far from fields of law.

Cornelius Allendyce *did* feel pleased with himself. How many men would have dared put this thing through the way he had? And how well it had all turned out; Madame somewhere seeking her "rest," living in her past, her mind undisturbed, Jimmie sailing away to get inspiration, and little Robin happy in the shelter of Gray Manor. Indeed, it had all turned out so surprisingly well that he could tuck it away, figuratively speaking, in the steel box in his safe, marked "Forsyth." Only he did not want to - he liked to think it all over.

Up to the time of finding Robin, girls were a species of the human race of which the lawyer knew little. He supposed that they were all alike - pretty, fun-loving, timid, giggly, prone to curl themselves like kittens, impulsive, and pardonably vain. He knew absolutely nothing of the fearless, honest, open-air girls, with hearts and souls as straight and clean as their healthy young bodies or that there were legions like little Robin and Beryl who, because they had been cheated of much that went to the making of these others, stood as a type apart. He only thought - as he went over the whole thing - that Robin's Jimmie was to blame for her being "different," leaving her alone so much and letting her take responsibilities way over her head; now she would enjoy the girlish pleasures that were her due. His sister Effie had supplied her with everything in the way of clothes and knick-knacks she could want; Harkness would keep old Mrs. Budge in line, Tubbs would go light with the school work - he had certainly made a point of *that*, and, when he could run up to Wassumsic again, he'd look over this little companion Robin had adopted. If she were not all that she ought to be (Miss Effie had somewhat disturbed him on this point) why, a change could be made; someone a little older and more cultured (Miss Effie's word) could be sent up from New York.

Upon this train of pleasant contemplation, enjoyed at intervals in his work, Robin's letter, written a few days after her dinner at Mrs. Lynch's, fell like a bomb.

"DEAR GUARDIAN," she had begun,

I am ever so sorry I haven't written for so long, but I haven't had a minute, really, truly. There are so many things to look at and to do. I am beginning to really love Gray Manor - it is so always and always beautiful. Mr. Harkness is a dear and is very good and tells me what to do many times when I am stupid and do not see for myself - like the finger-bowls. Jimmie and I never used finger-bowls. I don't mind the school work, though I simply can't keep up with Beryl. When you come up, I will tell you how wonderful Beryl is and all about her family. Her mother had a lovely dinner one night and Beryl took me. Beryl is going to be a great violinist, you know, and she is saving money to buy a real violin that will be all her own and take lessons. She will not let me do a thing to help her, which is splendid - I mean, for her to be so proud and brave, though I wish she would let me do just a little.

We have some very good times together, mostly taking lovely rides back in the hills to places Harkness tells us about and once we took our lunch and Mr. Tubbs and Harkness went, though Mr. Tubbs had dreadful neuralgia afterwards. Beryl and I read every evening. I love the books. I think I've been hungry for them all my life and didn't know it. We're playing a game to see which of us can read the most. We can play forever because one day we counted the books in the library and there are one thousand and seventy four and Harkness says there are more in Christopher the Third's room. Harkness has been telling us all about him and he showed us his picture - you know, the one in the Dragon's sitting-room (I apologize, in Aunt Mathilde's room) and he looked like a young prince, didn't he? How will Aunt Mathilde ever reconcile herself to a little insignificant, lame thing like me when she sees me?

Oh, I wish I could really *truly* meet my good Fairy somewhere - the one who forgot to attend my birth - and she'd give me one wish, I'd just ask for one. And that wish would be to G-R-O-W. I never cared before but now I want to be BIG. Oh, and wise! Mr. Tubbs will tell you how stupid I am. A Forsyth ought to be big and wise. You see, before this I have never thought of myself as a real true Forsyth - I've always just been Jimmie's daughter. But lately I've been thinking a lot about what a Forsyth ought to be and there are about a million questions I'd like to ask:

1. Ought Mr. Norris to let the Mills sink into a boneyard of antiquity?

2. What is the very most money I could spend all in one lump and can I spend it without telling anyone about it beforehand?

3. There's an empty cottage just below where the Manor road crosses the river and Williams says the Forsyths own

it. Can Beryl and I use it for a club?

Thinking of the questions makes me forget the other nine hundred ninety nine thousand, nine hundred and ninety seven, (I did that on paper) but please come to Gray Manor soon so that I can ask the rest.

Your loving Red-Robin.

P.S. The violin came and thanks ever and ever so much though Beryl says she will not call it hers for one little minute. But she most cried over it she loves it so and she makes the most beautiful music with it. I am dreadfully jealous because she won't even listen to a word I say now. She says she's living in the clouds. It's wonderful to have a big dream, isn't it? But I am starting one which I'll tell you when it's big enough."

Mr. Allendyce read the letter three times, stopping at intervals to polish his glasses as though they must be at fault. "What does this mean?" he exclaimed over and over. "What's up?"

Why on earth was Robin worrying her little head over the Mills and talking so absurdly about a boneyard? And why did she want more money? And who were these people with whom she had dined? And what did she and Beryl want with a club when they had all Gray Manor to play in?

Not able to answer any of these disturbing questions the poor man sought out Miss Effie - who, having been a girl, once, herself, ought to know something of the vagaries of a girl's mind.

Miss Effie felt very proud that her brother cared anything for her opinion. She nodded wisely and smiled reassuringly.

"Girl notions - that's all. Don't worry over the foibles of growing girls. It's one thing today and something else tomorrow."

The guardian was not so easily reassured. "But Robin isn't like other girls -" he began, with a disturbing recollection of Robin's highhandedness in engaging a companion.

"Tush! Bosh!" Miss Effie would not let him go on. "Girls are all alike under their skins. This poor kiddie's been starved for nice things and her sudden good fortune's gone to her head. She doesn't know the value of money, either; what'd seem big to her would be carfare for you. Give her more to do. And she ought to know some young folks."

Now Cornelius Allendyce beamed fondly upon his sister. She *had* comforted him. Of course, Robin's subconscious self was reaching out to touch the lives of others. In spite of their uncertain living she and Jimmie were of a sociable sort - he ought not to have expected that she would be content in Gray Manor with no outside interests.

"Couldn't that tutor get up a party?"

"That's a good idea, sister. I'll write to Tubbs. Probably the county's expecting something of the sort, anyway. I suppose it ought to be rather simple - she's so young and Madame Forsyth being away. I'll raise the child's allowance, too - let her spend it if she can, bless her heart."

His mind once more quite at ease, Cornelius Allendyce put Robin's letter into his pocket. He would write to her the next day and to Percival Tubbs. He ought to have consulted his sister sooner. Well, a guardian learned something new every day, he told himself, with a smile.

*   *   *   *   *

No one had suspected the torment of thought that racked poor Robin's head for the few days following the dinner-party. She had arisen that next morning with the firm resolve to "be" a Forsyth, but she did not know just what she ought to do first and there was no one to tell her. Beryl was no more sympathetic than she had been the night before and had answered her persistent questioning absentmindedly. However, unknowingly, she did give two helpful hints, upon which Robin seized gratefully.

"Mother says that what Wassumsic ought to have is a clubhouse like Miss Lewis' place in New York. Mother took care of that, you know. Miss Lewis is a wonder. She always declared children need fun just the way they need milk and *She* fixed it so that they got both."

"Oh, yes, there are ever so many boys and girls in Wassumsic only they're mostly working in the Mills. I'd have to work there myself only I've made Dale believe that I can do something - else. If I ever started in the old Mills I'd be like the others. That's the way - you begin and then you never know how to do anything different."

"I'm glad you're not there. I'm like - Dale. I know you'll be a wonderful violinist some day!" Robin never failed to say what Beryl wanted.

Beryl tossed her head. "I could have just settled down into a drudge, working all day and too tired at night to care what I did and saving just enough out of my pay envelope to buy me a hair-net but I wouldn't begin! I wouldn't! They can all call me proud and lazy but I'll show them - old Henri Jacques and Martini himself said I would! But I've had to fight to make people believe me - and I s'pose I'll have to go on fighting." To the egotism of sixteen years these words sounded very grand; it stirred Beryl to think she had fought for every advantage that was hers, to read the admiration in Robin's eyes. She had no thought of disloyalty in claiming the credit that really belonged to the little mother who had dreamed the dream first for her girl and then, through years of work and self-denial, had lived for that dream to come true.

After the arrival of the violin Beryl promptly lost herself in a trance of rapture that left Robin to her own pursuits. Only once the quite human thought flashed to her mind that Beryl might be a little bit interested in what *She* wanted to do but she put it away as unworthy for, she told herself, Beryl, destined one day to stand on a pedestal, could not be expected to bother with such every-day things as planning "fun" for the Mill children.

So Robin left Beryl with her beloved instrument and went alone to talk to Mrs. Lynch who was so startled at her unexpected coming that she kissed her and called her "little Robin" before she realized what she was doing. That, and the fact that she found Mrs. Lynch working in the shed where big Danny could not hear them, made it much easier for Robin to talk and talk she did, so rapidly and so imploringly that Mrs. Moirahad to interject more than once: "Now wait a bit, dearie. What was that again?"

Robin wanted to know about how many Mill children there were.

"Oh, bless the heart of you, it's no one but the doctor himself can tell you that! They slip in and out of the world as quiet like. But Mrs. Whaley says the school's so full that her Tommy can only go afternoons."

Robin remembered Beryl pointing out a dingy brick building as the schoolhouse. It had a play-yard enclosed on three sides with a high board fence, disfigured by much scrawling. It had seemed an ugly spot. She thought of that now.

"And what do the girls - the girls like me - do?"

"Oh, they mostly work. After work? Well, they help at home and do a bit of sewing maybe and some have beaux and they walk down to the drug store and hang around there visiting, though Beryl doesn't. 'Tisn't much of a life a girl in a place like this has," and Mrs. Moira's sigh was happily reminiscent of her own girlhood in open clean spaces, "it's old they grow before their time."

"They don't have much fun, do they?" Robin asked.

Mrs. Lynch looked at her curiously. "Fun? They work so hard that they haven't the gumption to start the fun. But it's so big the world is, Miss Robin, that it can't all be rosy. Sure, there has to be some dark corners."

"Mrs. Lynch, if - if - someone started the fun for the girls - would they like it?"

"Why, what's on your mind, dearie? The likes of you worryin' your little head over things you don't know anything about!"

Robin could have cried with vexation. She *must* make Mrs. Lynch understand her - Mrs. Lynch was her one hope. She gave a little stamp of her foot as she burst out: "I'm little but that's no reason I can't think of things. I'm fifteen. Dale said that the Forsyth's didn't care and they ought to care - and I'm a Forsyth. I want to know everyone in the Mill neighborhood and how they live and what they do. And I want them to have - fun. Beryl said your Miss Lewis said everyone ought to have fun. I - I don't know just how to begin - but I'm going to."

Mrs. Moira patted her hand. To herself she was saying: "The blessed heart of her, she doesn't even know what she's talking about, poor lamb," but aloud: "That you shall and if I can help you, I will."

Robin's eyes glowed. "Oh, *thank* you. You don't know how hard it is for me to think just what to do. Lovely plans keep popping into my head and then I think maybe they're silly and I can't tell about them - I just have to feel them. I'd like to begin with the little children. If my guardian says we may, can't we open that old cottage down by the bridge and make it into a - a sort of play-house? There could be a play-yard and next spring we could make gardens and we could fix one room up with pretty pictures and have books and games - and a fireplace and window-seats. Oh, *does* that sound silly?" Robin brought her enthusiasm to an abrupt, imploring finish.

"Dearie me - no." There were no reserves in Mrs. Moira's approval. With an imagination as quick as Robin's she saw the old cottage - it was a charming old house, snuggled under elms, half-covered in summer with rambling vines and pink blossoms - alive with romping, happy-voiced children, some poring over pretty picture-books, others listening to a story, some working in a garden - some just tumbling about on the soft grass in a pure exuberance of youthful joy.

"We'll call it the House of Laughter. I always think of names before anything else. And maybe, some day, the older girls - girls like me - will use it, too. I'd like to begin by knowing little Susy Castle."

Mrs. Lynch promised to take her the next day to the old village where Susy lived.

"I'll come down right after our school work is over. Beryl won't mind because she'll want to practice. And, please, Mrs. Lynch, don't tell Dale, will you?"

Mrs. Lynch demurred at this, for already she had been looking forward to telling Dale about Robin and her plans. But Robin stood firm.

"You see I may spoil everything and he'd think I was just stupid. I don't want him to know - yet."

Robin walked back to the Manor with a light heart. Her world that had always seemed so small, bounded on its every side by Jimmie, now suddenly assumed limitless proportions and beautiful possibilities. There was so much to be done and so much to think about. Tomorrow she would see Susy Castle; maybe other boys and girls.

Lights were twinkling from some of the windows of the Manor. Robin paused for a moment at the bottom of the long ascent to "love" the Manor in its purple cloak of gathering dusk. That first Forsyth who had broken ground for this gray pile had chosen well; the hill upon which the house had been built stood apart from the other hills, loftily commanding the village and valley.

"It looks just like a grand old lady holding off her skirts so's not to touch anything," Robin thought, now, whimsically.

As though to crown her day's progress toward "being" a Forsyth, Robin found a letter from her guardian awaiting her. Cornelius Allendyce had written it keeping in mind his sister's advice not to notice a girl's "foibles" - "it's one thing today and another tomorrow."

> "... I am delighted that you are happy and finding so much to occupy your time. Do not worry about your lessons. Not all   knowledge is confined within the covers of school books. (He had read that somewhere and thought it came in very pat, now.) How about some sort of a party. You ought to know the people of the country before the winter sets in. Think it over and decide what you want. I will double your allowance if you haven't enough. If you need a club to make you happy, help yourself. Don't worry about the Mills - let Norris do that. I'll run up to Wassumsic very soon and answer as many questions as you may wish to ask. Until then, I am
>
> Devotedly yours,
> CORNELIUS ALLENDYCE."

"Beryl - read this! I may use that old cottage. I believe my guardian'll do everything I ask when he understands. He's a *dear*!"

Beryl came slowly down from her "clouds."

"Robin - listen to *This* vibrato!"

CHAPTER XIII

SUSY CASTLE

The Forsyth Mills had built Wassumsic - in truth, Wassumsic *was* the Forsyth's Mills. It had had its beginning in that first small mill where the first Forsyth worked in his shirt-sleeves; a cluster of houses had sprung up close to the river, a store, more houses, more stores, a tavern, a church, a school. And as the Mills grew, so grew the village. For themselves the Forsyth family had built the stone house on the hill, that looked, indeed, like a grand old woman holding off her skirts from contamination. And that lofty apartness had always been the attitude of the Forsyth family to the workaday life in the village.

The growth of the village had been toward the railroad so that the first Mill houses had been left by themselves "up the river" and were commonly known as the "old village." They were so old that they were not worth keeping in repair and so close to the river that they were damp the year round and for these very good reasons were offered to the mill workers at a low rental. Many of the mill workers - such as Dale - looked upon them as a disgrace to the Mills and felt a hot anger in their hearts when they thought of them - but unfortunates like the Castles were glad to move into the worst of them.

The short walk from the Mills to the old village skirted the river and was overhung with a double row of willows which, on this wintry day, cast long purple shadows. Robin, walking along it with Mrs. Lynch, thought it lovely and solemn - like a cathedral aisle. But when they stopped before a low cottage, one window nailed across with boards where the panes were missing, the front door propped in place by a rotting rail tie, tin cans and frozen refuse littering the strip of yard, and Mrs. Lynch said "This is the house," she wanted to cry out in protest at the ugliness. They had to pick their way around to a back door upon which Mrs. Lynch knocked. Several moments elapsed before the door swung back a little way, a round black eye peered at them cautiously, and a shrill voice piped "whachy'want?"

"I s'pose that's Susy," thought Robin, her heart skipping a beat with a terror of shyness.

Mrs. Lynch's pleasant: "We want to see Granny," admitted them. Robin, blinded for the first moment of coming into the darkness of the room from the bright sunshine outside, stumbled over a chair and in her confusion mumbled some incoherent answer to the shrill cackle of welcome that came from the shrunken bit of humanity bending over a small stove.

"Poor Granny doesn't understand who you are," explained Mrs. Lynch, in an apologetic whisper, touching her head significantly. "Come here, Susy," and she motioned the staring child to her. Susy approached with the hang-back step of a child or a dog not always certain of what he may get but Mrs. Lynch magically produced a round cookie, fat with currants, and Susy sprang at her with a quick leap.

The room was heavy with stale air and bare of any comforts. A tattered First Reader lay on the greasy floor, unwashed dishes cluttered the bare pine table, on every available shelf and in every corner were piled old cans and bottles and half-filled paper bags. On a what-not in the corner a faded bunch of pink paper roses drooped over a cracked vase. The wallpaper, its ugly pattern mercifully faded, was fantastically streaked from the dampness, in one corner the ceiling plaster had fallen and newspapers had been tacked over the laths to keep out the cold.

A sickening revulsion, a longing to escape into the sweet crisp air swept Robin. She shrank away into a corner for fear the dreadful old Granny might touch her. But she *must* say something! She had come here for a purpose - to know Susy.

At that moment Susy's voice pealed out in a merry, piping laugh - because she had put her small finger into her cookie and pulled out a fat round currant! And something in the laugh touched the spark to the mothering instinct strong in Robin's young heart - the mothering instinct that had caused her bitter anguish over Cynthia's loss, that had taught her how to care for her Jimmie, and had given her strength to run away from her Jimmie that he might have his "chance." She forgot the dirty surroundings, the old Granny in her rags and her crown of wispy gray hair, she saw only the child's face, lightened with joy, and laughed with Susy as Susy held out the currant on the end of an uplifted - and very dirty - finger.

The ice broken, Susy made friends quickly. She leaned her thin little self against Robin's knee and stared with rapture into Robin's face. Like Granny she could not seem to realize that Robin was a Forsyth; to her she was "a big girl" and big girls did not come to the house now that Sarah had died. She timidly touched Robin's soft coat sleeve with a rough, sticky hand and poked at the bright buttons of Robin's blouse, her eyes round with wonder.

Afterward, after Robin and Mrs. Lynch had, with some difficulty, broken away from Susy's clinging and Granny's childish lamentations, and were walking back through the "cathedral aisle" Robin gave herself a little shake as though to rouse herself from some nightmare.

"Oh, Mrs. Lynch, it's dreadful!"

"What, dearie?" Mrs. Lynch had been thinking that Granny

Castle couldn't be one of the Castle's of her old-country county.

"That place. Are they all like that? How can they live?"

Mrs. Lynch hesitated a moment and there was a perceptible tightening of her tender lips.

"Well, dearie, people *have* to live - life goes on in spite of things. Maybe poor old Granny wishes real often it'd been her that had been taken instead of that poor Sarah. Things weren't so bad for them when Sarah lived - they say. She was an up-and-doing girl and kept things nice though she had to work hard to do it, poor little thing. It's in the hospital that old woman should be with some one to wait on her and keep her warm. No one but little Susy -"

"I forgot all I'd planned to say! Susy looked so cold, Mrs. Lynch. I hated my nice warm clothes."

"Oh, Susy was warm enough. She's a bright child, she is. When she's a bit older things will ease up."

Robin remembered what Beryl had said of the girls in Wassumsic having nothing else to do but go into the Mills. Susy would grow older and take Sarah's place. But what if she didn't want to? What happened to the "big girls" who didn't want to go into the Mills? Robin could hear Beryl's contemptuous: "Why they haven't a chance in the world." Well, anyway, someone could make the Mills so nice that the girls would *want* to work in them. "I wish I were big!" cried Robin with such passion that Mrs. Lynch, not knowing her train of thought, had a sudden qualm at taking a sensitive little thing like Miss Robin to poor old Granny Castle's.

"Now, dearie, don't you worry. Things come out somehow - in the next world maybe for the Granny Castles, but they do. Now that idea of yours of fixing that cottage -"

"Oh, I forgot to tell you! My guardian says I may. At least he said that if I wanted a club, to help myself, and that must mean he consents. He's a dear. Have you time to go there with me now and just peek into it? I'm sure we can get in."

"I'll take the time," cried Mrs. Moira with an interest as eager as Robin's. "I'll just drop in and tell my Danny when we go past - it's so lonesome he gets when I'm slow coming."

Robin's House of Laughter looked a little deserted standing alone in the shadow of the hillside, gaunt branches creaking over its low roof, the ends of the trailing vines whipping restlessly against the gray clapboards. But Robin and Mrs. Lynch saw it as they wanted it to be - neatly painted, its windows curtained, its yard trimmed, its doorstep dignified by a broad inviting step, and flanked by a trellis for the rambling rose vine. The door opened for them in the most promising way and they tiptoed into a big bare room with two windows at one end looking out over the hills and river.

"Isn't this nice?" cried Robin in delighted staccato. "It's just made for what we want. Look - a fireplace!" To be sure, it was nothing more than a gap in the wall. "And these darling windows. We can put a seat way across, all comfy." She promptly saw, in her mind, Susy curled upon it with a beautiful picture book and a handful of cookies. "Oh, let's see the rest. Look, a cunning kitchen. The children can play cooking. And this room - what can we use this room for?"

Mrs. Lynch was thinking rapidly. Because of her experience with Miss Lewis she saw possibilities way beyond Robin's eager planning – class rooms where the older girls could learn other trades - a domestic science class in the kitchen for the mothers - a sewing room, a library full of instructive and entertaining books, and the big living room where the children could gather after school hours, and the men and women and big boys and girls in the evening. And a playground outside - and gardens.

"Can't we fix it up right away?" Robin's eager questioning

brought her sharply out of her dream to a practical realization that all the House of Laughter had as endowment was an unselfish girl's enthusiasm.

"Harkness will help if I ask him and maybe Williams, too. And Mrs. Williams."

"It's quite tidy for standing empty so long," mused Mrs. Lynch, sweeping the bare rooms with an appraising eye. "That stove's good as new under the rust."

"Oh, you *will* help, won't you? I can't do anything without you."

"That I will, Miss Robin." Mrs. Moira promised with no thought of the added tax it must be on her energy. "It's a beginning everything has to have and you get your Harkness man and some brooms and some soap and we'll have your little House of Laughter ready to begin in no time."

A half hour later Robin burst upon Beryl absorbed in her practicing.

"Oh, *please* listen," she cried and without waiting for encouragement poured out her precious plans. Beryl obediently listened but with an odd surprise tugging at her attentiveness - this Robin seemed different, full of a fire that was quite new, and all over fixing up that old place for the Mill kids. To Beryl, wrapped in her own precious ambition, that seemed a ridiculous waste of energy. However she concealed her scorn, affected a lively interest and put in a few helpful suggestions.

"Mr. Tubbs has been hunting for you," she suddenly informed Robin. "I heard him talking to Harkness about a party. Your guardian's written to him, I guess."

"Oh, *dear*!" cried Robin, in dismay. She remembered what Mr. Allendyce had written to her. A party would be terrible!

"I should think you'd think it was fun - and with all your pretty clothes. It's exciting meeting people, too. If *I* were you -"

Beryl simply wouldn't finish - there were so many things she would do if she were Gordon Forsyth, she could not begin to name them.

Robin's doleful face betrayed her state of mind.

"What will I have to do?"

"That depends upon what kind of a party it is." Beryl felt flattered that Robin should appeal to her. "And I should think you'd have the say. *I* certainly would. Receptions are stiff and dinners aren't much fun. I think a dance -"

"But I can't dance. And I never went to a young party in my life!"

"Well, you're Gordon Forsyth, now, and you'll have to do lots of things you never did before," reminded Beryl, a comical sternness edging her voice.

An hour before, in her empty House of Laughter, poor Robin had thrilled at the thought of "being" a Forsyth; now, alas, her heart sank to her boots under the weight of these new obligations she must face. Nor was she cheered when Mr. Tubbs found her and laid his plans before her. Mr. Tubbs, short of memory, always carried his thoughts on neat little slips of paper over-written with memoranda. He fluttered some of these now before Robin's eyes and Robin saw that they contained lists of names.

"A party - your guardian is quite right - we were remiss - of course Madame would have wished - in the old days - it must be at least an at-home - yes, an at-home - I have found the cards of the best people of the county in Madame's desk - Harkness will know who of them have died - yes, an at-home, say from four to seven - Mr. Allendyce and his sister will come to help you receive - I will talk to Budge - yes -" Mr. Tubbs rarely finished a sentence. He always spoke as though he were thinking memoranda aloud, and punctuated his words with little tugs at his silky Van Dyke beard.

Robin had a rebellious impulse to snatch the fluttering lists from his long fingers and tear the "best people of the county" into tiny bits but she remembered what Beryl had said about a Forsyth having to do many things, smothered a sigh, and said meekly: "I don't know much about parties."

"My dear young lady, experience will teach you. They are important - yes, for one of your station - important as your books. I will see Budge - about the date - yes."

"Old grandmother!" cried Beryl, as Mr. Tubbs went off in search of the housekeeper. "An at-home!" She mimicked his precise tones. "Of all the tiresome things. He'll invite a lot of doddering old women who'll come and look you over *This* way!" Beryl lifted an imaginary lorgnette to her eyes. "Why didn't you say you'd like a regular party and just have young people - there's a boys' school only ten miles from here and it would have been such fun. Of course I couldn't have come down but I could watch you -"

"Beryl Lynch, you *are* coming down or I won't stir one foot. You shall pick out one of my dresses and we'll make it longer or something. And I think a party with boys I don't know would be lots more terrible than an at-home. All I hope is that he makes the date soon so that it will be over with."

Percival Tubbs, inwardly much annoyed at having the peaceful routine of his days at the Manor thus disturbed, was as anxious as Robin to have the party over with. After due deliberation with Mrs. Budge he fixed the date for a day two weeks ahead. Mrs. Budge insisted she needed that much time to make "things look like anything."

Budge and Harkness welcomed the party as a beginning of the "change" they had prayed might come to Gray Manor.

"It'll be some'at like old times," Harkness had declared.

"That chit won't look like much," (poor Budge had not yet forgiven Robin for being a girl) "but it'll make talk if she ain't shown. Talk enough for Madame going away like she did. I've half a mind to get out the gold plate. That old Mis' Crosswaithe from Sharon'll be over here the first of any, peeking around and she ain't going to see how things are going to sixes and sevens. No one else ain't either or my name ain't Hannah Budge. It ain't." And Budge squared her shoulders as a challenge to an inquisitive world.

Harkness, while he anxiously watched the weather, grew loquacious over the old times. "This house has known great parties, missy," he told Robin. "The best lydies from miles 'round coming in their carriages. The Crosswaithes, from Sharon, before old Mr. Crosswaithe died. And the Cullens and the Grangers - she as was the daughter of a gov'nor. The Manor was the finest place in the county and things were done right here and as gay as could be." He launched forth on a long description of Christopher the Third's eighteenth birthday party. "He come up from school, missy, with his friends and the young lydies come from New York and some from these parts and the house was as gay, what with flowers and palms and music and their talk. And the young master's table was laid in the conservatory - and the olders sat in the dining-room and Held come from New York - the best caterer, missy -"

Robin and Beryl listened with breathless interest - Robin with a moment's vision of that handsome lad laughing and talking with the "young lydies from New York." How dreadful, she thought, that only a few months after that brilliant affair he should have been killed - he would have been about twenty-four, now - and would have been such a splendid Forsyth, while she was so small and insignificant.

"These automobiles are all very well, missy, but if it snows -" and Harkness scowled through the window at the darkening sky.

"Do you mean, if it snows - no one will come?"

"I'm not thinking that, missy, but not so many - the Grangers and their young people."

Robin refrained from saying she hoped it *would* snow, for if Harkness and Budge enjoyed fussing over the dreadful party she did not want to spoil their anticipation.

The entire house seemed ridiculously astir over the approaching event; extra help came from the village, the air throbbed with the hum of vacuum cleaners, chairs and tables were beaten with a frenzied thoroughness, tables polished, everything dusted. Certainly, no one *was* going to see that things were going to sixes and sevens!

Robin and Beryl busied themselves making over one of Robin's dresses for Beryl, a process to which Beryl consented only after a stormy scene and tears on Robin's part.

Robin's plans for her House of Laughter had to be tucked away for the time, and when she sighed now and then over her ripping and stitching it was because she'd so much rather be making frilly, crispy curtains for those little windows.

CHAPTER XIV

A GIFT TO THE QUEEN

By no means had the girls forgotten their Dowager Queen of Altruria. They talked of her often; Beryl usually in a speculative vein. Had she brought the court jewels with her? Did that dreadful Brina kneel on one knee and kiss the hem of her garment? Did she ever wear her crown?

Royalty meant much more to Beryl than it did to Robin, for Beryl attached to it a personal interest. Would she not, as sure as anything, sometime play before crowned heads by royal command? Sometimes, lying wide-eyed in the dark, she pictured herself at such a moment, gorgeously gowned, and delightfully disdainful of the bejeweled, becrowned, stately kings and queens and little princelings, dukes and duchesses and earls and countesses, all hanging on the exquisite notes she drew from her strings. After she finished they would forget their crowns and things and fall upon her in a sort of humble adoration. Beryl shivered exquisitely, she could make the picture so very real! Now, when she dreamed, the queens and duchesses looked like the mysterious mistress of the house by the Rushing Water.

Robin thought of their Dowager Queen of Altruria as perhaps being a little lonely, sometimes. With everyone, now, watching the weather in anxious dread of a snowstorm, it occurred to her that such a storm would shut the little house near the Rushing Water off from the world.

"Beryl, let's go and see our Dowager! It may be the last time we can until Spring. I'd like to take her something, too. Something Christmasy. Christmas is only two weeks off and think how dreadful to spend Christmas all by yourself."

Beryl thought both the visit and the gift a fine idea and set her wits to working to contrive an offering suitable for one of the Dowager's station in life.

She suggested helping themselves to what the Manor had to offer, for, certainly, Robin, being a Forsyth, had such a "right."

"Flowers and fruit and maybe a book. It would never be missed and you could take one of these that hasn't anything written in the front. See, here's a collection of Dante's poems - it's as good as new. And who'd ever want it with all these other books here?"

Beryl's reasoning seemed logical and Robin put aside a tiny doubt she had as to her right to "help herself" to even a very small volume. Some day she could explain to her Aunt Mathilde that she had given it to a nice old lady who lived all alone.

The girls filled a huge basket with luscious fruit from Budge's storehouse, and gay flowers from the conservatory, and concealed the little book under the bright foliage. They decided, after much deliberation, to let Williams into their secret, and show him their offering, so that he would surely consent to drive them to Rushing Waters.

"We'll just about get it in before the snow comes," agreed Williams, scanning the sky with that anxiety to which Robin had grown very familiar. "A Queen, you say? Well, what do you think of that!" He laughed uproariously.

"We're not exactly *sure*, but we have our suspicions," corrected Beryl in a freezing tone.

"And please don't tell a soul because we really have no right to force ourselves on her if she wants to hide away," begged Robin.

Williams promised with a chuckle. "Funny kids," he said to himself, enjoying, nevertheless, the adventure. "I'll do the sleuth stuff in the corner store while you two are interviewing the Duchess - I beg pardon, the Queen."

The girls left Williams, as he suggested, at the little store, while they, tugging their basket between them, found and followed the path by the Rushing Water. It was as alluring as ever - berries still clung to the undergrowth, gleaming red against the dark of the fir trees; the dead leaves underfoot crackled softly as though protesting their intrusion; there was a whirring of wings and always the rush of the water.

"I'd forgotten how spooky it was," cried Beryl, drawing in her breath.

"I hope she won't be sorry we came."

This time Robin knocked. As before, Brina opened the door a little way. When she saw the two girls she scowled, but stepped backward, announcing their presence in crisp German.

The mistress of the house rose a little hastily from the table before which she was sitting. She was dressed, now, in a warm, trailing robe of soft velvet, a band of ermine circling her neck and crossing over her breast, where it was held in place by a brooch of flashing gems. At sight of her visitors her face softened from haughty surprise to a resigned amusement. Robin broke the silence.

"May we come in? We thought we'd like - that maybe you'd like -" Oh, it was dreadful to know what to say, when all the time you were thinking she really was a Queen!

"You have stumbled upon my little house again? Come in and

sit down. Brina and I do not often have callers; you must pardon us if, perhaps, we are a little awkward in our hospitality. Caesar, lie down *He* is glad to see you! I have been looking over a book of colored prints of old cathedrals. Would you like to pull your chairs up to the table and look at them with me?"

Beryl blinked knowingly at Robin as much as to say: "Isn't that just what an exiled Queen would be doing?" The prints were rare and exceedingly lovely and Robin noticed that they had come from a New York gallery. Their hostess told them of some of the quaint cathedral towns and the stories of the cathedrals themselves. Robin, who had an inherited appreciation of beauty, listened eagerly, putting in now and then a question or a statement of such intelligence that the "Dowager Queen" studied her with interest.

Beryl, thrilled by the ermine and the gleaming brooch, did not care a fig about the cathedrals but sat back in a rapture of speculation. There seemed something in the stately head with its crown of white hair, vaguely, tantalizingly familiar; she must have seen pictures of the Queen of Altruria somewhere. She watched each gesture and fitted it to her dream. This Queen who seemed really truly friendly now and almost human, might go back some day to Altruria, wherever that was, and of course, when *She* toured Europe, or maybe even when she was there studying, she could go and stay at the Palace just like a relative. It would be fun to visit in a palace and smile at all the fuss and crowns and things because you were an American and didn't believe in them.

"Oh, we forgot our basket!" cried Robin, suddenly darting to the door where Brina had, with a sniff, dropped their precious offering. "We brought these - for a Christmas greeting."

"They are lovely," cried the "Queen" with sincere delight, her eyes drinking in hungrily the beauty of the exotic blossoms - for Robin and Beryl had helped themselves to the best the Manor had. "And fruit - ah, Brina's heart will rejoice. What is this?" Her slender, shapely hands fussed over the wrappings of the book, while Robin and Beryl watched.

"Why -" The Queen turned the book over and over, her face bent so that its expression was hidden. The girls' delight gave way, now, to concern - the Queen held the book so long and with such curious intentness that they wondered, anxiously, if there were anything about Dante's verses displeasing to a Queen of Altruria. "You never *can* tell about those jealous kingdoms over there!" Beryl said afterwards.

After their hostess had "most worn the book out staring at it" she lifted her eyes and fixed a curious gaze upon her visitors.

"This is a rare little treasure," she said in a queer tone. "And may I not know how it came into your possession - and who you are?"

Robin's heart jumped into her throat. What had they done? It had looked like any book except that the leather of the binding seemed softer than most books and smelled very nice and there were beautiful colored illustrations inside - but the Queen said it was a rare book and was wondering where they had gotten it. Perhaps they had helped themselves to the Manor's most precious book! She gulped, looked frantically at Beryl, who, guessing her intention, gave violent signs of warning, to which she paid no heed.

"Why, I'm Robin Forsyth, and this is Beryl Lynch who lives with me at the Manor. We took the book from the library there becaus there are ever and ever so many, and we thought you might be lonely - when winter comes - and enjoy it."

"You are Robin Forsyth?" The old lady said the words slowly.

"My real name is Gordon Forsyth, but I've always been called Red-Robin. I'm living at Gray Manor now - over in Wassumsic. My father - he's not one of the rich Forsyths, you see - is an artist and he's travelling with Mr. Tony Earle, who writes, you know. I wish you could come to the Manor." Robin's heart was light now, having, by confession, cleared itself of its moment's dread, and she rattled on, quite oblivious to Beryl's scowl and the Queen's searching scrutiny. "It's lovely and old. Madame Forsyth, my great-aunt, isn't there, though - at least now. She's - she's travelling. We have a tutor and I have a guardian who lets me do about what I please. You see, first my aunt and my guardian thought I was a boy - the Forsyths have always *been* boys; and it was a dreadful shock, I guess, when my guardian found out I was a girl - and such a small girl - and lame, too. I think, though, he's forgotten that, now. But the housekeeper never *will* forgive me. And my great-aunt doesn't know, yet. I wish for her sake, I could change myself into a handsome young man like young Christopher Forsyth who died - but I can't, so I'm just going to be as good a Forsyth as I can and make up to them all for - being a girl."

"Whom do you mean - 'them all?'" asked the Queen. She had dropped into a chair and turned her head toward the fire, in very much the same attitude she had held upon their first visit.

Robin, encouraged, squatted on the hearth rug, the big dog beside her, and clasped her hands over her knee.

"Oh, I don't mean just Madame Forsyth and my guardian, though I don't think he cares, now, or that cross old housekeeper; I mean - all the Mill people. You see the Mills have grown very fast and there are lots and lots of people working in them, but Mr. Norris, he's the superintendent, is very old-fashioned and he'll never improve things." Robin racked her brains to recall Dale's and Adam Kraus' exact words. "He's letting the people live in awful houses and they don't have any fun or - or anything. And Dale - he's Beryl's brother - says they'd work much better if they had everything nice. *He* says the Forsyths don't care, that they just think of the Mill people as parts of a machine to make money for them, and not as human beings. Why, there was a girl, Sarah Castle -" and Robin, her tongue loosed, told eloquently of Sarah Castle and of Susy and Granny and the old cottage "up the river," and then - because it made it seem so real to tell about it - of her House of Laughter.

"Of course," she finished, "if I were a boy I could do much more - or even if I were big. You see, there's been what Mr. Harkness calls a gloom over the Manor for a long time; and my great-aunt's been so sad over that that she couldn't think of anything else - and maybe I'll be doing something if I just show the Mill people that a Forsyth, even if she's only a girl, *does* care - a little bit. Don't you think so?"

At her appeal the Dowager Queen turned such a haughty face upon her and answered in such a cold voice: "I'm sure I do not know," that Robin turned crimson with embarrassment. Of course, a Queen could not even be remotely interested in the Manor and the Mills - especially if she had to worry over a whole kingdom herself. She had been silly to rattle on the way she had!

Brina, quite unknowingly, came to the rescue with a tray of cakes and a pot of cocoa.

Their hostess, her annoyance put aside, smiled graciously again, and poured the cocoa into little cups while the firelight flashed from the brooch on her dress. Brina went back and forth with heavy tread, sullenly watchful of her mistress' smallest need. The girls sat close to the table upon which still lay the book of cathedral prints and sipped their cocoa and ate their cakes. The wintry sun shone in through the curtained windows, giving the room, with its pale glow, a melancholy cheerfulness.

"Must you really go?" asked their hostess, politely, when, a half-hour later, Robin and Beryl exclaimed at the lateness of the hour.

"Why, we never meant to stay so long! It has been so nice." Robin wondered, if she held out her hand, would the Queen take it? She ventured it with such a shy, appealing movement that the old lady clasped it in hers, then dropped it abruptly, as though annoyed by her own impulsiveness.

"The afternoon has passed very pleasantly for me." The Queen's voice was measuredly polite. "I thank you for thinking of me - in my out-of-the-way corner, and bringing me such lovely gifts." Her eyes turned from the flowers which Brina had put in a squat pewter pitcher to the book which lay on the table. Then she turned to Robin and levelled a glance upon her which held a queer challenge.

"If you succeed - with your - what did you call it - House of Laughter, let me know, sometime. I shall be most interested in your experiment."

"Then she *was* listening," thought Robin, wondering at the bitter tone in the woman's voice. "Maybe she's so lonely and so unhappy she hates to think of laughter."

"Well, Red-Robin Forsyth, you certainly did spill everything you knew and a lot more besides," cried Beryl, when the two were alone. "As if a Queen cared a fig! I tried to head you off a couple of times." Beryl laughed scornfully. "It was *funny!*"

Robin still smarted from her recent embarrassment; she did not relish Beryl's laughing at her.

"We had to talk about something," she cried in defence.

"Well, if you'd given me a chance I'd have talked about things that are happening in Europe. Sort of led her on, you know, so's maybe she'd give herself away. *That's* what *I* wanted - to find out something about *her* instead of telling all about ourselves. Here she knows everything about you and you notice she didn't say one word about herself! The whole afternoon's wasted and we might as well not've gone at all. I wanted to get something on her so's maybe - some day -" Disgusted, Beryl broke off abruptly, quickening her step to show her companion her displeasure.

Robin limped in silence after her; she *had* talked too much, the Queen was probably laughing at her now - and Beryl was angry and disgusted.

Beryl forgot her moment's displeasure, however, when Williams imparted to them the "dope" he had on the "Queen-dame," gleaned from the old storekeeper.

"Old Si says the 'queer party' bought that house off up there last fall suddenly and moved up from somewhere or t'other with a truck load of stuff. The Big-gun, beg pardon, I mean the Queen, came herself, with some sort of a body-guard in an enclosed car, that went away after it'd landed them in the woods. Si's sore, I suppose, because they get 'their vittles sent up from New York' - though I don't know as I blame them from what I saw in his store. Says the 'queer party' walks through the village sometimes, but she's always with her body-guard and a big dog, and wears a heavy veil 'like them furrin' women'." Williams chuckled as he tried to give to his little account the touches Si had put into it.

Beryl caught Robin's hand in an ecstasy of delight. "There. *that* settles it as sure as anything. I'd like to write to somebody in Washington and tell what we know and maybe we'd get a reward. Royalty most always has a price on its head," Beryl finished grandly.

Robin wanted to protest at the thought of there being a price on that snow-white head, but not certain as to how far she had been restored in Beryl's favor, she refrained, and merely smiled in assent to Beryl's excitement.

"We've got to hurry back if we beat that cloud yonder," declared Williams, nodding toward a gathering bank of dark clouds in the western sky, and the mention of snow brought back to the girls the approaching party.

It did snow - long before Williams reached the Manor, so that the car was covered; throughout the dinner Harkness went again and again to the window to peer out, always turning back with the worried announcement: "It's still coming down." And at bedtime Robin, peeping out, saw a world blanketed white. Even Mr. Tubbs laid his neuralgic head upon his soft pillow with the regretful thought: "Now the Grangers cannot come. A pity. Yes."

CHAPTER XV

THE PARTY

The household at Gray Manor looked upon the heavy fall of snow with varying emotions. Harkness lamented loudly: "It might 'a held off for Missy's party. If it was the old days - well, the county lydies could a' come in their sleighs. All right as far as the post road goes, but the Grangers -"

Downstairs Budge rejoiced that the Grangers might not come. "Eyes like a ferret that woman has and like as not she never got over our boy's going. She'd say things *was* going to sixes and sevens, with a little thing no bigger'n a penny in our boy's shoes - she would. But I'd like to know who ever'll eat all the stuff I'm fixing!" The house cleaned to a fine polish from attic to cellar, Mrs. Budge had turned her attention most generously to the food.

"Why does everyone care about Mrs. Granger?" asked Robin, of Harkness, when even Percival Tubbs regretted, with a sigh, that Mrs. Granger might not find it possible to come.

"Well, you might say she's next lydy to Madame herself," explained Harkness. "In the old days her people and the Manor people were thick like and visited backward and forward. And there was talk of young Christopher some day marrying the young lydy, Miss Alicia. I hear tell his death was a sad blow to them. They haven't been coming much to the Manor since, but we laid it to Madame's queer ways and the gloom."

"Will the others be able to come? Won't Mrs. Budge have *lots* too much food?"

"Well, you might say most will make it, for they keep the post roads open. We'll hope for the best, missy," he added, interpreting Robin's anxious questioning as an expression of disappointment.

But Robin's sudden concern over the party had nothing to do with the coming of Mrs. Granger or anyone else. As she had stood in the window, her nose flattened against the pane, staring out at the snowy slopes, she had been suddenly inspired by a beautiful plan. She turned to Beryl.

"Can something be sent up from New York in a day?"

"Depends." Beryl answered shortly. "What?"

With one of the lightning-like decisions, characteristic of her, Robin decided not to take Beryl into her confidence - just yet.

"Oh, I was thinking. Something about my party. I'll tell you - later."

Beryl stared at Robin a little suspiciously - Robin looked queer, all-tight-inside, as though she'd made up her mind to do something. It was the new Robin again. Oh, well, if she didn't want to tell -

After luncheon Robin donned her warm outer garments and slipped out of the house while Beryl was practicing. To carry out her plan, now fully grown, she must send a telegram and see Mrs. Lynch.

Two hours later, flushed and excited, she hunted down Mrs. Budge, whom she found mixing savory concoctions in a huge bowl.

"M'm, how good things smell," she began, to break down the hostility she saw in Budge's eye, "Is that for the party?"

"'S going to be," and Budge stirred more vigorously than ever.

"Mrs. Budge, will there be enough food for - some extra ones - I've invited or I'm - going to invite?"

Budge dropped her spoon. "Well, no one ever went hungry in *This* house," she answered crisply. "May I ask who *your* guests are?" Budge permitted herself the pleasure of a meaning inflection on the "your."

"Well, I'm not quite sure - yet, only I wanted to know about the food -" Robin retreated step by step toward the door, her limp exaggerated by the movement. "I'm waiting for word from my guardian."

"*Robin*! Humph," Budge flung at the door as it closed upon the girl. "If it wasn't that this house depended on me I'd drop my spoon and walk out this minit, I would, or my name ain't Hannah Budge. Guests! Like as not some of these Mill truck."

More than the snowstorm threatened the success of Robin's "at-home." For Cornelius Allendyce was suddenly prostrated by a bad attack of sciatica. And his sister declared she could not leave him; at such times only her patient and faithful ministrations eased his intense suffering.

"I'll telephone to Wassumsic right away and don't you worry," she begged of him, "they'll get along somehow or other."

"They'll have to," the guardian growled, between groans.

But before Miss Effie could telephone, Robin's telegram came. Cornelius Allendyce opened it with indifferent fingers, read it, then rose upright with such suddenness that a loud cry of pain burst from him.

"Will you listen to this? That child wants me to express fifty sleds to the Manor, at once! Read it and see if I've gone crazy."

"There, there, lie still, Cornelius - I don't care if she wants fifty sleds or fifty hundred. Send them to her and wait until you're well to find out if she coasted on all of them or wanted them for kindling wood. There - I knew it'd make your pain worse. Wait - I'll warm this!" All solicitous, for her brother's face had twisted in agony, the sister dropped the telegram and busied herself over her patient.

Her advice seemed good. "Well, send them. Tell them to rush the order," he groaned, then gave himself over to his suffering with, somewhere back in his head, the thought that there was quite a bit more to being a guardian than he had calculated.

So while Harkness and Budge and Mrs. Williams, pressed into service, made the old Manor festive with flowers and pine boughs, Robin completed the plans for her part of the party, and confided to Beryl that fifty of the Mill youngsters were coming to the Manor to coast on the sloping hillside.

"Robin Forsyth, what ever will they all say?"

"Who?" demanded Robin, with aggravating innocence.

"All the guests. Why, Robin, you're hopeless! You simply can't get it into your head that the Forsyths are different from - the Mill people."

"They're not. And we haven't time to argue now. They're coming - a lot of them. Your mother invited them for me through the school teacher - you see, there wasn't time for me to, because I didn't know where the younger children lived. My guardian has sent on the duckiest sleds - all red. Williams brought them up and they're out in the garage. He's going to take charge of my part of the party."

"Does Budge know?"

Robin hated to admit that she had been afraid to tell Budge. She flushed ever so slightly. "N-no. At least I told her there were some extra coming. Oh, Beryl, *don't* act as though you thought everything was going to be a failure. I thought - as long as there was going to be this stupid old reception here and lots of nice food, it was the *only* time to have a party for the kiddies, for Budge would never cook a crumb if it were just for them. I wish my guardian were here - I *know* he'd understand."

"Where are they going to eat?"

"The ladies? Oh, the children. I've told Harkness to put a table in the conservatory and make it Christmasy."

"You're clever, Robin. Harkness will do it for you - but, oh, he'll hate it; I can hear him - 'things aren't like they used to be.' As my father'd say-you're killing the goose that lays the golden egg, all righto. Budge will tell Madame, sure's anything."

"What do you mean?" asked Robin quietly, a little gleam in her eyes.

"Why, stupid, the Forsyths aren't going to stand for that sort of thing. They'll send you back -"

"Beryl, do you think I'm staying here for the Forsyth money - or - or care about it? I came here so that Jimmie could go away without worrying about me. When he comes home I shall go back to him, of course."

"Leave Gray Manor?" Beryl's voice rang incredulously.

"Of course. I like it here and there are lots of things I want to do, but when Jimmie comes back - if he wants me -" her voice trembled.

Beryl stared at Robin as though she saw a strange creature in the familiar guise. "You *are* the queerest girl. You don't seem to care for the things money can get for you!" She had to pause, to pick her words. "Why, if *I* had the chance - all the advantages, and taking lovely trips, and the fun. You could go to one of these girls' schools and play tennis and golf and ride horseback! And always have pretty clothes!" The bitter edge to Beryl's voice betrayed how much she would like these things.

"Would you desert your mother and - and Dale for things like that? Would you?"

In her relentless dreaming, in her sturdy ambitions, Beryl had never put such a question to herself. She had simply never seen them in her picture. She evaded a direct answer now.

"They'd want me to!"

"Of course they would. Mothers and fathers are like that. Just unselfish. But you wouldn't give your mother up for anything. I know you wouldn't."

Beryl turned away from Robin's searching eyes. In her innermost heart - an honest heart it was - she was not quite sure; her life had been different from Robin's, she had been taught to want fine things and go straight for them; so had Dale. If getting them meant sacrificing sentiment - well, she'd do it. So, perhaps, would Dale (and Robin thought Dale perfect). But she couldn't make Robin understand because Robin had never wanted anything big - Beryl always fell back upon this comforting thought.

"Well, you'd better get Harkness in line and don't get so interested in your kids that you forget Mrs. Granger. She *is* coming - they telephoned that the road is open."

Robin dropped an impulsive kiss on the top of Beryl's head to show her that, no matter how much they disagreed, they were good friends, and went off in search of Harkness.

The appointed hour for the reception found the Manor and its servants ready. With myriad lights, gleaming from candles and chandeliers, reflecting in the polished surfaces of old wood and silver and bronze, the air sweet with the scent of pine and flowers, the old Manor had something of the brilliancy of other days. But, in sad contrast to the old days, now poor Budge watched the extra help from the village with a dour and suspicious eye and Harkness, dignified in his faded livery, made the "extra" table in the conservatory as Christmasy as he could, with a heart heavy with doubt as to the "fitness" of Missy's whims. Robin, in her Madonna blue dress, looked very small in the stately drawing room. There Percival Tubbs patiently explained, for the hundredth time, with just what words she must greet her guests, as Harkness announced them; and Robin listened dutifully, with her thoughts on the hillside beyond the long windows where already red sleds were flying up and down the snowy slope and childish voices were lifting in glee.

True to Mrs. Budge's predictions, Mrs. Crosswaithe, from Sharon, arrived first. Robin saw masses of velvet and plumes and a sharp, wizened face somewhere in the midst of it all. She forgot Mr. Tubbs' careful teaching, said "I'm pleased to know you," instead, and held out her hand to the tall, thin, mannishly dressed young woman behind Mrs. Crosswaithe, who, though Robin did not know it, was Mrs. Crosswaithe's daughter.

For an hour the guests arrived in as steady a stream as their high-powered cars could carry them through the heavy roads. The Manor had not been opened like this for years and the "best people in the county" took advantage of the opportunity to look for signs of failing fortunes, to see the "girl" who had come to the Manor, and to find out just where Madame was travelling. Thanks to Budge's heroic work no one discovered any sign of change in the old house; their questioning only met with disappointment, and Budge's food was of much more interest than the young heiress who, they decided, was a pretty little thing but much too small for her age.

Robin shook hands until her arm ached, mumbled the wrong thing most of the time which, however, did not seem to make any difference with anyone, and kept one eye longingly on the window, and one ear listening for the shouts outside which were growing louder and louder. She seized an opportunity to go to the window and watch, so that when the great Mrs. Granger arrived Mr. Tubbs had to, a little sharply, recall her to her duty.

"Isn't she - awful?" whispered Robin to Beryl, as Mrs. Granger, after condescendingly patting Robin's hand, swept on.

"She thinks *she's* so grand, but she ought to see the Queen!" Which observation would have enraged Mrs. Granger, had she heard it, for she had felt particular satisfaction in her dress and hat, sent on, only the day before, from the most expensive shop in New York.

"Miss Alicia didn't come - she's in California. Say, Robin, there's a Granger boy, 'bout eighteen. Maybe that's why my lady Granger's so sweet to you."

"Silly!" Robin flung at Beryl in retort. "Oh, dear, can't I go out to my own guests now?"

Robin and Williams had planned that the children should be admitted to the conservatory through a side door, leaving their outer garments in a vestibule. So, when everything was in readiness for them, Harkness gave the sign, and Williams herded his noisy troupe to the house.

Many of the older guests had been present at that memorable birthday party on young Christopher's eighteenth birthday and they recalled now, over their salad plates, the brilliancy of that affair and touched upon all that had happened since in the way of change. Mrs. Granger displayed much emotion.

"*that* made a picture I will never forget!" and she nodded toward the glass doors, curtained in soft silk, which led from the dining room to the conservatory and which Harkness had carefully closed. "I wonder if I might just peep in? Ah, the memories. My dear Alicia and that handsome boy -" she touched a lacy handkerchief to her eyes.

Several who had overheard her followed Mrs. Granger to the closed doors and stood behind her as she opened them. And their eyes beheld a sight so different from that birthday party that they stepped back in amazement, Mrs. Granger lifting her lorgnette in trembling fingers.

Youngsters of every size and of every degree of greed crowded around the long table, the "Christmasy" decoration of which had already been pulled to pieces by eager reaching hands. Faces, still red from the crisp air and streaked where dirty coat sleeves had rubbed them, beamed across the heaping plates, busy fingers crammed away the goodies. One small boy half-lay across the table; another stood in his chair, his frayed woolen cap set rakishly back and over one ear. On each excited countenance a shadow of suspicion mingled with the joy, a fear that the same magic which had brought it might snatch all this strange and lovely fun away. Harkness watched at one end of the table, Williams at another. And in their midst sat Robin.

"Well, I never!" murmured Mrs. Granger. Her exclamation was drowned, however, in the babble of youthful sound let loose upon the "best people of the County" by the opening of the door. "Miss Gordon is going in for the pretty charity thing, is she?"

All might have gone well even then - for Harkness had a stern eye on everyone of Robin's small guests - had not little Susy seen her beloved "big girl" slip through the group at the big glass doors. Susy was the youngest of the children there; she did not go to school regularly enough to feel at home with the others, she had refused to slide, and, at the table had not really begun to enjoy herself until Robin had sat down next to her, put her arm around her and coaxed her to eat the food on the plate before her. The food had turned out to be very good and

Susy had crammed it down with her fingers, regardless of fork or spoon. Now her "big girl" had slipped away, she was alone, that man at the end was staring at her, panic seized her, a mad longing to escape, anywhere - preferably back to the shelter of the "big girl's" friendly arm. She slid down from her seat, her eyes wildly sweeping the room; Harkness, like an ogre, guarded one end of the table, Williams' bulk stood between her and the outer door; there was only the one way, through the glass doors. Head down, she ran swiftly the length of the conservatory and bolted into the little group of people watching from the dining room door. Someone big blocked her way. With frightened hands she pushed at her.

"Want Granny! *Want Granny!* Get 'way! Uh-h-h!"

"The dreadful little thing!" someone said.

Robin, hearing the shrill cry, rushed to the rescue, and, kneeling, gathered poor weeping Susy into a close embrace. Over the child's tousled head she smiled nervously at her staring guests.

"Poor little thing, she's shy!" Then, feeling Susy quivering in her clasp, she whispered something magical in her ears. It was only: "Robin will keep tight hold of your hand, Susy-girl, and you needn't be a bit frightened and by and by, if you're quiet, we'll fill a bag of goodies for your brother and Granny." But it soothed Susy at once, and, clinging to Robin's hand, she stared at the guests from the shelter of Robin's skirts.

There was a little stir among the "best people of the County" - a renewal of the chatter, high-pitched, pleasant nothings, and side remarks, in careful undertones.

"Certainly, not a bit like a Forsyth."

"I rather think Madame doesn't know what is going on here."

"Fancy entertaining these little persons and Mrs. Granger with the same spoon, so to speak."

And, in a corner, Mrs. Granger was raging over the damaging imprint of two sticky hands on the delicate fabric of her costly gown. For her's had been the bulk that had stood between Susy and her "big girl," and Susy had been eating chocolate marshmallow cake with both hands!

Mrs. Granger had come to Gray Manor with the intention of coaxing Miss Gordon to spend Christmas at Wyckham, the Granger home. But, as she made ineffectual dabs at the greasy spots on her skirt with her silly little handkerchief, she put such a thought quite away from her mind.

"Brat!" she cried under her breath, angrily, and from the way she glared at Robin and Susy no one could have told which of the two she meant.

CHAPTER XVI

CHRISTMAS AT THE MANOR

Christmas without Jimmie was, for Robin, a thing not to think about. And from Beryl, inasmuch as that young lady affected a stoical indifference to the holiday, she could get little sympathy. Beryl had shocked her with the heresy: "Christmas is just for rich people, anyway."

"It is not. Oh, it isn't," Robin had cried in remonstrance. But she could not tell of her and Jimmie's happy Christ-days without giving way to the tears which, at the thought, scalded the backs of her eyes. It had not been alone the holly and pine of the shop windows, or the simple gifts Jimmie's loyal and more fortunate friends brought, or the usual merry feast that had made them happy; it had been a deep and beautiful understanding of the Infinite Love that had given the Christ-child to the world, that Love which surpassed even Jimmie's love for her or hers for Jimmie, and that was hers and everyone elses. She had felt it first when, a very little girl, she had gone, once, with Jimmie into the purple shadows of a great church, where the air was sweet with incense and vibrating with the muted notes of an organ. She had stood with Jimmie before a little cradle that had seemed beautiful with gold and precious colors but, when she looked again, was a humble thing of wood and straw, and what she had thought so bright was the radiance of candles and the reflection from the many-colored windows. Then she had looked at the cradle more closely and had found that it held a beautiful wax babe. When Jimmie

Jane Abbott

tugged at her hand she had reluctantly turned away. At the same time a shabby old woman and a little boy, who had been kneeling nearby, arose, and the old woman and the little boy had smiled at her - a *different* smile and she had smiled back. On the way home Jimmie had explained to her that the Gift of the Christ-child was the great universal gift and belonged to everyone, the world over. She knew, then, why the shabby old woman had smiled - it was over the Gift they shared.

"Christmas is for *everybody*," she finished.

"Well, all it means to me now that I'm big," pursued Beryl, "is stores full of lovely things and crowded with people lucky enough to have money to buy them. And talking about how much everything is. I heard a woman once saying she had to spend five dollars on her aunt because her aunt always spent five dollars on her. That's why I say Christmas is for the rich - it's a sort of general exchange and take it back if you don't like it or have half a dozen like 'em, or put it away and send it to some one next Christmas. Miss Lewis, at the Settlement where mother worked, gave a book to a lady one Christmas and got it back the next, and the leaves weren't even cut."

Robin laughed in spite of her disapproval of Beryl's heresy. "There *are* different kinds of Christmases, Beryl, and I'll show you," she protested, then and there vowing to make the Christmas at the Manor a merry one, in spite of odds.

"Well, the nicest thing *I* know that's going to happen is that Rub-a-dub-dub is going home," retorted Beryl.

"That *is* nice, but there'll be even nicer things. Let's invite your mother and Dale for dinner and have a little tree and we'll make all sorts of foolish things to put on it."

To Beryl this did not sound at all exciting but Robin loved the thought of sitting with Mrs. Lynch and Dale and Beryl, like one happy family, around the long table. She'd ask Harkness to cut pine boughs and a nice smelly tree, which she and Beryl would adorn with gifts that had no more value than a good laugh.

And she would coax Harkness to get Williams and his nice wife to help open and clean the House of Laughter. She'd like to have it a Christmas gift from her to the Mill children.

She found Harkness ready for her wildest suggestion. He had confided to Williams and Mrs. Budge that he felt sorry for little Missy alone in the big house on Christmas.

"A lot of pine and holly, Missy, and the old place won't look the same. A tree - of course there'll be a tree! Whoever heard of Christmas without a tree. Many's the one I've cut with the young master; he'd have no one but Harkness do it, for he said I always found the best trees."

But the old man's head began to whirl a little when Robin explained about the House of Laughter and the dinner that must be "different." She had to tell him again and again, until her tone grew pleading.

"I'll help you, Missy, only I'm a little slow just understanding. It'll come, though, it'll come. Williams will give a hand and his wife maybe, and I'll tell Mrs. Budge about the Christmas cakes and things. It'll be as merry a Christmas as old Harkness can make it, Missy."

"Oh, Mr. Harkness, you're a dear," Robin cried, with a look that made the old man's heart almost burst with affection.

"But I won't tell Hannah Budge any more than she has to know," he thought, as he went off to do Robin's bidding.

With Williams and his wife and his wife's sister, who had married the telegraph operator at the little station, pressed into the work, the empty cottage at the turn of the road took on rapid changes. Windows were opened, doors were thrown wide, letting in the sweet cold air; under the magic of strong soap and good muscle the old wood-work shone with cleanliness; the faded walls lost their melancholy. Harkness and Williams hauled down a load of wood and piled it high by the back door; Mrs. Lynch transformed the rusty stove into a shiny, efficient, eager thing.

Williams, who was very clever and would have been a carpenter if he hadn't been a chauffeur, built tables out of rough boards and, in the living room, put up shelves for books and the window seat Robin wanted.

Robin and Beryl flew about in everyone's way, eager to help and generous with advice.

"There, I'd say things were pretty nice," exclaimed Williams, at the end of the sixth day of work, stepping back to survey with satisfaction the chair he had made out of "odds and ends."

"But it doesn't look like what we want - yet!" Robin glanced about dolefully. "It needs such a lot to make it homey. Where'll we ever get it all?"

"Now, Miss Robin, Rome wasn't built in a day, as I ever heard of," protested Harkness, a smudge over his nose and two long nails between his teeth. "I guess there's truck enough in the attic up there at the Manor to fill this house and a dozen like it."

"Oh, Mr. Harkness, may we use it? Or - just borrow it until my aunt returns? Can we?"

Harkness exchanged glances with Williams. Harkness knew that it had long been Mrs. Budge's custom to make a two day trip to New York during the week preceding Christmas. They could take advantage of her absence.

"Well, I guess we can borrow enough, Missy, to do." And no one thought of smiling at his "we" for, indeed, everyone there felt that he or she had a share in Robin's House of Laughter.

But even stripping the Manor attic of its "truck" did not satisfy Robin and the day before Christmas found her House of Laughter lacking in the things she wanted most.

"It ought to have jolly pictures and ever so many books and pillows and nice, frilly curtains," she mourned, wondering how much they would cost and how she could ever get them.

On Christmas morning, Harkness dragged to Robin's door a box of gifts from her guardian. Most of them Miss Effie had selected, as poor Cornelius Allendyce was still confined to his room, and that good-hearted woman had, with a burst of real Christmas spirit, simply duplicated each gift, for, though she wasn't at all sure, yet, that this "companion" of Robin's choosing was the refined sort Robin ought to have, nevertheless she was a girl like Robin and Christmas was Christmas. Beryl appreciated the thoughtfulness more than she could express and when she found a little book entitled "Old Violins" and *only one*, she hugged it to her with a rush of happy feeling.

Later in the morning Mrs. Granger's chauffeur arrived with a great box of bon-bons in queer shapes and colors. Neither Robin nor Beryl had ever seen anything quite so extravagantly contrived.

"She paid a fortune for *that*," declared Beryl, appraisingly. "She must have forgiven Susy for spoiling her dress. Or maybe she's thinking of her son again. Let me read the card. 'Hoping you will coax that nice Mr. Tubbs to bring you to us before my youngsters go back to school - ' Didn't I tell you, Robin?"

"I won't go," Robin answered briefly, pushing box and card away with a gesture that disposed of Mrs. Granger and her son. "Now we must trim the tree."

Harkness, true to his boast, had found quite the straightest, princeliest balsam in the nearby woods. Its fragrance penetrated and filled the old house. The girls went about sniffing joyously, carrying in their arms all sorts of mysterious objects made of bright paper. Harkness, oddly dishevelled and excited, balanced on a stepladder and fastened the gay ornaments where Robin directed.

Beryl had laughed at the idea of having a Christmas tree without the usual tinsel and glittering baubles. But after Robin and Harkness had worked for a half-hour she admitted the effect was very Christmasy and "different."

"You're awfully clever, Robin," she declared, in a tone frankly grudging. "You make little things count for so much - like mother."

"I think *that's* a compliment. And speaking of your mother, Beryl Lynch, we have just time to wash our hands and faces and change our dresses before she comes. Oh, hasn't this day simply flown? And *hasn't* it been nice, after all? Isn't Harkness darling - look at him." For Harkness, his head on one side, a sprig of holly over one ear where Robin had put it, was surveying the effect of an angel which Robin had made of bright tissue paper and which he had carefully hung by the heels.

"That kite looks as real as can be, Missy."

Giggling, the girls rushed away to make ready for what Robin declared (though she had been much hurt by Dale's refusing to come) the nicest part of Christmas.

Belowstairs Mrs. Budge was directing Chloe with the last touches of the Christmas feast.

"That's the prettiest cake I ever saw if I do say so," she cried, patting the round cherry which adorned the centre of the gaily frosted cake. Then, lest she grow cheerful, she drew a long sigh from the depths of her bosom. "But, cake or no cake, I never thought I'd live to feed Mill persons, coming to our table like the best people. Things plain common. It ain't like the old days - it ain't."

"The old days are old days, Hannah Budge," rebuked
Harkness, who had come into the kitchen. "Mebbe our little
lydy's ways aren't our ways but it isn't so bad hearing the
young voices and you'll admit, Mrs. Budge, that that's a fine
cake and there'd be no cake if Missy wasn't here, now, won't
you?"

"I haven't time for your philosophizing, Timothy Harkness.
With things at sixes and sevens I have enough to do!" But Mrs.
Budge's tone had softened. She *had* not made a Christmas cake
(at sixteen Hannah Budge had taken the prize at the County
Agricultural Exhibit for the finest decorated cake, and she had
never forgotten it) since Master Christopher the Third had left
them. And she *had* enjoyed hearing young voices and eager
steps in the old house and had caught herself that very
morning, as she helped Chloe stuff the turkey, singing:

"Oh, com-m-me let 'tus a-dor-r-re Him."

Chloe's last delectable dish for the dinner eaten, Harkness
drew back the folding doors to reveal the Christmas tree in the
conservatory. And Robin, waiting for Mrs. Lynch's "oh" of
admiration, gave vent herself to a delighted cry of surprise for,
at the foot of the tree, so still as to seem a graven image, sat
little Susy, cross-legged, staring in wrapt contentment at the
bright ornaments.

"Susy, you *darling*, where in the world did you drop from?"
Robin rushed to her and knelt at her side.

Without moving her eyes so much as a fraction of an inch,
Susy indicated the side door of the conservatory as her means
of entrance. In one hand she clutched a soiled ragged picture
book, on its uppermost page the colorful illustration of "The
Night before Christmas." Susy had not forgotten the magic of
that side door which had opened for her upon a feast beyond
her wildest imaginings; if there were a place on earth where

that Christmas tree of her picture could come really true it must be at the "big girl's." Alone she had bravely climbed the hill to the Manor to find out.

Not a word could Robin's questioning drag from her.

"You shall stay here as long as you want," Robin finally declared, popping a round bon-bon between the child's trembling lips. "We needed a little girl to sit at the foot of that tree, didn't we?"

At Robin's command, Harkness played the role of Santa. The girls had fashioned all sorts of nonsensical gifts out of paper and cardboard and paste; no one was forgotten. Mrs. Lynch declared herself "as rich as rich" with bracelets and a necklace made of red berries. Mrs. Budge, forgetting, when Robin held a sprig of mistletoe over her head and daringly kissed her wrinkled cheek, that "things was going to sixes and sevens," laughed until her sides ached at Harkness in his silly clown's cap. Robin and Beryl, with much solemnity, exchanged purchases each had secretly made at the village store and Robin could not resist adding: "Dare you to send it to me next Christmas."

Beryl had to admit, deep in her heart, that Robin had managed a Christmas full of joy that had nothing to do with stores full of lovely things and crowded with people lucky enough to have money to buy them. Never having thought much about the Christmas spirit, she had no name with which to explain Mrs. Budge's awkwardly kind manner - even to her, or her mother's unusual animation, or why the picture of little Susy, still rooted to the tree, clasping a great paper doll in her arms, made her glad all over. But after a little she disappeared, and presently, from the library, came the strains of her violin, low, pulsing with a deep emotion, now a laugh, now a sob, climbing higher and higher until they sang like the far-off, quivery note of a bird, flying into the heavens.

A deep hush fell over the little group of merrymakers.

Harkness coughed into his hand. Mrs. Budge fussed around the spacious belt of a dress for a handkerchief and, finding none, surreptitiously lifted a corner of her apron. Mrs. Lynch caught her throat with a convulsive movement as though something hurt it. Robin, watching her, slipped her hand into the mother's and squeezed it.

"Don't go," she whispered when the music suddenly ceased. "Beryl's funny. She likes to be alone when she plays."

"I never heard her play - like *that*!"

"Oh, Beryl's wonderful!" Robin smiled happily in her faith. "She makes that all up, too, 'cause she hasn't any music. She's going to be the greatest violinist in the world. Hush!"

Beryl had begun a lilting refrain, as though a mother laughed as she sang a lullaby. It had in it a familiar strain which carried little Mrs. Moira back to Beryl's baby days. Then the lullaby swung into the deeper tones of a Christmas anthem and again into a tempestuous outburst of melody, as though Beryl had let loose all at once the riotous feelings that surged within her.

Just as the last note died away a bell pealed through the house. Because it was still Christmas, really being only nine o'clock, everyone looked for a surprise. And a surprise it was, indeed, when Harkness placed an impressive envelope in Robin's hands and said that a stranger had brought it to the door.

"He looked like one of these motorcycle men, but before I could as much as say 'Good evening' he was off in the dark."

Robin studied the address, which was printed. It gave no clue whatsoever. Nor was there anything else on the envelope. She broke the sealed flap, with an excited giggle. Five crisp banknotes fell out.

"For goodness' sake," cried Beryl, staring. "Who ever sent them?"

"TO MISS GORDON FORSYTH. Please use this money for your House of Laughter. I am deeply interested in your experiment. Frankly, I do not believe it will work; but if it does my little contribution will be well spent; and if it doesn't, my own conviction will be justified.

YOUR FRIEND NEAR THE RUSHING WATER."

Beryl squealed with delight. "How *larky* to have her remember every solitary thing you told her, Robin - even what we called her house. What are you going to do with it all? I wish *I* could get money like that."

Robin stood staring at the letter - not at all jubilant over the unexpected gift. "I wish she hadn't said she didn't believe the experiment would work. It *isn't* an experiment and it *will* work. I'm not *trying* anything, am I?" appealing to Mrs. Lynch, who hastily assured her with a "No, dearie." Then Robin gathered up the bank-notes.

"Though I did wish we had more nice things for the house and now we can get them. But isn't this an awful lot of money?" For she had seen a one and two ciphers in a corner of one bank-note. "I never had so much in my life."

At this Mrs. Budge sniffed and, the Christmas celebration apparently abandoned in the excitement of the strange letter, she departed kitchenward.

Harkness volunteered to escort Susy and Mrs. Lynch back to the village. In a twinkling the house had quieted so that the girls' footsteps, as they climbed the stairs, resounded strangely.

Robin leaned for a moment against the banister and looked back into the shadows of the great, dimly-lit hall.

"Listen a moment, Beryl! Can't you hear tiny echoes of voices and laughter? Don't you s'pose even the things we think and feel get into the air, too - and linger?"

Beryl tugged at her arm. "Oh, come on, Robin. You make me creepy. You'll be seeing ghosts in a moment. I want to have a good look at that letter. *Wasn't* it a surprise, though?"

But after a close study of it, Beryl threw the letter down in disappointment. "Not so much as a tiny crown on it! I'll bet she had someone write it for her, too. It looks all big and scrawly - like a man. Anyway, Robin, you ought to keep one of the bills as a souvenir."

CHAPTER XVII

THE HOUSE OF LAUGHTER

The day after Christmas, and for many days thereafter, Robin counted over the five precious bank-notes. She knew with her eyes shut each line and shading of their fascinating decoration. She kept them in a little heart-shaped box that had been a favor at a studio party she had gone to with Jimmie a few years ago.

Their magic opened possibilities for her House of Laughter; curtains - cushions - books - pictures - games, why, she could have all the things she had wanted so much to complete her little cottage. And behind her eager planning was a thought she kept shut tight away in her heart. If there were any money left - by careful buying - the Queen would surely want her to give it to Dale to perfect his model. For had not Adam Kraus and Dale both said that the little invention would make everything at the Mills better? She would present her gift to him at the "opening" of the House of Laughter. Mrs. Lynch had assured her Dale would be there. Under cover of the general merriment she would find an opportunity. She went over and over, until she could say them backward, the few words with which she would make him accept the money.

Beryl, not knowing what was going on in Robin's mind, declared she fussed an awful lot over samples and lists for anyone who had so much money to spend and Mrs. Lynch encouraged her economy because, she said, "'Twas likely as not

the roof'd leak in the Spring and shingles cost a lot, they did."
When Robin declared the lovely rose-patterned cretonne too
expensive, Mrs. Lynch helped her dye the cheese cloth they
bought at the village store a gay yellow. And she wisely
counselled Robin to let her write to Miss Lewis (remembering
the simplicity of the Settlement House where she had worked)
and ask her to send up a few suitable pictures and the right
books with which to begin. "*She'll* know, dearie."

While the final preparations were going rapidly forward, Mrs.
Lynch took pains to spread the news of the House of Laughter
through the Mill Village by the simple medium of taking a cup
of tea with Mrs. Whaley and telling her all about it. "It's better
it is than the written word," she explained to Robin, who had
worried over just how the Mill people were going to know
about their plans. "And when you send the cute little cards
around it'll be in crowds they come, you mark me."

"Don't you think everything'll be ready by Saturday night?"
Robin asked eagerly.

Percival Tubbs, for one, hoped everything would be, for he
had not been able to hold Robin to serious study since the
holidays. And poor Harkness had developed a stitch in his
back hanging the pictures Miss Lewis sent and laying clean
white paper in cupboards and on shelves.

Though Beryl had not cared particularly whether the windows
of the living room of the House of Laughter were hung in rose
or yellow, and laughed when Robin chose a scarlet-robed
picture of Sir Galahad, because he looked as though he were
seeing such a beautiful vision, to hang over the shelf Williams
had built as a mantel, she felt a lively interest in the festivities
which were to open the House to the Mill people. Robin let
her help in planning everything to the smallest detail.

The children were to come in the afternoon and play outdoors
with their sleds and indoors with the books and games, eat
cookies and cocoa and depart with beautiful red and blue and

yellow balloons. In the evening the young men and women and the fathers and mothers were to gather in the living room and play games and sing and maybe dance and lock at the books and make lovely plans and admire everything. There would be sandwiches and coffee for them, too. And Robin would make a little speech, telling them that the House of Laughter was all theirs to do what they wanted with it and that the key would always hang just behind the shiny green trellis. Robin had demurred at this last detail, shrinking in horror at the thought of a "speech," but Beryl had insisted that she really must because she was a "Forsyth."

Then Robin wrote and sent to each of the Mill houses cards inviting them to come to the House of Laughter on Saturday night.

And, everything ready, she counted a precious two hundred dollars left in the heart-shaped box. That, with what she had not spent from her ridiculously big allowance, seemed a fortune.

Saturday dawned a crisp, cold, bright day, promising to the expectant sponsors of the House of Laughter, all kinds of success. But at twelve o'clock a little group of mill workers, chosen by their fellows, went to Frank Norris, the Superintendent, and asked for higher wages and better living conditions, Adam Kraus acting as their leader. It was not the first time these complaints and requests had been laid before the superintendent - but now, in the hearts of the hundreds of men and girls who hung around the yards long after the noon whistle blew, a new hope kindled, for there had never before been a man among them who could talk so convincingly as Adam Kraus or could more effectually make old Norris realize that they all knew now, to a man, that they could get more money almost anywhere else and work and live like decent human beings. Adam Kraus had opened their eyes. He was their hero - for the moment. As he came, somewhat precipitously, from the office building they gave a quick shout that died, however, with a menacing suddenness, as they saw his failure written on his angry face. They pressed about him, eager for details, but he would tell them nothing beyond a curt admission that he had not been able to make Norris listen.

"I say, go to the Manor!" cried a man who had not been at the Mills more than a month.

A strapping girl, with a coarse prettiness, laughed a mocking strident laugh that expressed the feelings of the crowd even more than the louder curses around her. The workers slowly dispersed, in little groups, talking in excited, angry tones. Dale Lynch detached himself from one of these groups and walked on alone, a frown darkening his face; nor did he shake off his absorption even after he sat down at the table to eat his mother's good Saturday meal - overcooked for standing.

"Has Adam been to Norris again?" asked big Danny.

Dale nodded. It was not necessary for either his father or mother to ask the outcome of the call. "Norris wouldn't listen to a word. I've been wondering if Adam is right - about the way to get this."

"He ought to know more'n you do," flared big Danny, who loved something upon which to vent his own rancor.

"I suppose." Dale admitted, eating with quick, absent-minded gulps. "I'd like to be the head of these Mills - I'd see both sides and make the other fellow see, too."

"Sure, it's wonderful you'd be," murmured Mrs. Lynch, caressingly.

"Well, I'm about as far from it as I am from being President of the United States. Adam has a better chance - if he ever gets his way. *There's* a leader."

Mrs. Lynch cut a generous portion of apple pie in a silence that said plainly she did not agree with her boy. Dale ate the pie, wiped his lips, pushed back the plate.

"The Rileys have got to move up the river."

"Dale, you don't say so?" Mrs. Lynch was all concern now. The Rileys were neighbors. Tim Riley had fallen down an unguarded shaft at the Mills and had hurt his back. Mrs. Lynch had helped Mrs. Riley care for her husband and had grown very fond of the plucky little woman. "Why, it's his death he'll get with the dampness up there, and those blessed little colleens."

"Well, they've got to go. Riley can only work half-time now and he can't afford one of these houses."

"Oh, dear, oh, dear," sighed Mrs. Lynch. "Don't tell Robin," she begged. "It's so happy the child is with her House of Laughter, as she calls it and - Dale, she's a different Forsyth."

"She's just a kid," he answered, in a tone that implied Robin could have little weight against the impregnable House of Forsyth.

But a few hours later, when, with the coming of night into the valley, the last tired youngster departed from the House of Laughter, balloon on high, the "just a kid" fell to restoring the House to its original perfection with a vim that seemed as tireless as her spirits.

"*Wasn't* it a success? Didn't the children have a wonderful time?" she begged to know, with all the happy concern of a middle-aged hostess. "Are you dreadfully tired, Mother Lynch? Because tonight's the real test." She stopped suddenly and leaned on her broom, her face very serious. "I do hope the big girls will like it. I wish the Queen hadn't said she didn't believe our - experiment would work. Why *won't* it work? Don't grown-ups like to be happy just as much as children - when they get a chance?"

Mrs. Lynch had no answer for Robin's wondering. "Queens don't know about things in this country," Beryl, instead, assured her. "These books are just about ruined. I thought Tommy Black would eat up this Arabian Nights."

"That shows how much they want them! I don't care if they *do* eat them." Robin was too happy to be disturbed by anything. Wasn't her beautiful plan in the process of coming true? And didn't she have her money in her pocket all ready for Dale's grasp?

She had brought flowers from the Manor which she arranged on the tables and the mantel under her beloved Sir Galahad. These, with the mellow glow of the lamps and the sun-yellow of the curtains, and the gleams of red from the shiny stove, which had to do for the fireplace Robin had wanted, and the brilliant scarlet of the Sir Galahad, all served to soften and lend beauty to the faded bits of carpeting and the shabby furnishings brought from the Manor attic.

"I do think everything's lovely and it's just because you've all been so kind about helping," Robin declared, viewing the room with pride. "I hope ever so many people'll come and that they'll believe it's theirs. But, oh, Beryl, don't you think we could make them know without my saying a speech?" And Robin shivered with nervousness.

"Of course not," Beryl answered with cruel promptness. "Anyway, as long as you thought about all this you ought to get the credit." Beryl had no patience with Robin's "blushing-unseen" nature. "It'll be easy, anyway. You just ought to know how I felt the day Mr. Henri took me to play for Martini. Why, my knees turned to putty. But then, *that* was different. Listen, there comes some one now! I'll stay in the kitchen until the sandwiches are made."

Dale opened the door and Adam Kraus followed him in. Then, while Robin, two bright spots of color burning in her cheeks, was showing them the new books, a group of mothers arrived, stiff and miserable in their Sunday best, and she shyly greeted them. When another knock sounded Mrs. Lynch took the women in charge so that Robin might welcome the newcomers. They were four of the Mill girls and they crowded into the room, staring curiously about them and at Robin, whose greeting they answered awkwardly. Spying Adam Kraus, they rushed to him with noisy banter and laughter that had a shrill edge.

Robin, left alone and without the courage to join either group, watched the girls as they gathered about Adam Kraus and Dale. Suddenly panic seized her. She fought against it, she told herself that everything was going all right and that in a few moments more people would come, and these girls, who looked at her so rudely from the corners of their eyes, would forget about her and have a good time. From the kitchen, where Harkness was presiding, came the first faint aroma of coffee, and Beryl and Mrs. Williams were piling dainty sandwiches on plates as fast as their quick fingers could make them. Mrs. Lynch and the mothers seemed to be gossiping contentedly at one end of the room but Robin wondered why they talked so low, and why Mrs. Lynch now and then glanced anxiously in her direction; once she heard something about "the Rileys" and an imploring "hush" from Mother Lynch. Adam Kraus and the four girls were urging Dale to do something and Robin saw a big girl with bold black eyes lay a persuasive hand on Dale's arm, which Dale shook off almost rudely. Robin hated the girl, and wished she had the courage to break into the circle and drag Dale away from her, instead of standing in such a silly way in the kitchen door with her tongue glued to the roof of her mouth.

And, oh, why *didn't* more people come? What was the matter?

After what seemed to Robin an interminable time, though in fact it was only a few minutes, Adam Kraus moved toward her, trailed by the four girls. "I've got to run along, Miss Forsyth," he said in his easy, soft voice. "There's an important meeting in the village. You've fixed a nice little doll house here."

The girl with the black eyes, standing just back of Adam Kraus' shoulder, laughed - a scornful laugh.

"Too bad the Rileys can't move here!"

The Rileys again! Robin flushed at the girl's laugh and hateful eyes, tried to answer Adam Kraus and to beg them all to wait until Harkness brought in the coffee, but found her throat paralyzed and her feet rooted to the spot. The Mill mothers saw Adam Kraus and the girls start for the little hall and hastily moved in that direction themselves.

"Oh, *don't* go!" Robin managed to cry, then, moving after them, "Mrs. Lynch, make them stay. Why, I wanted this to be a *party*, to - to – This is your House of Laughter! I -" She struggled desperately to recall the words of the "speech" Beryl had declared perfect and to keep from breaking down into tears before these hard, staring eyes.

The black-eyed girl elbowed her way out from behind the others, casting a quick look at Adam Kraus as though for his approval. "I guess you named this house all right, Miss Forsyth. It *is* to laugh! But there ain't many of us that know all poor little Mamie Riley's stood, and cares about her the same way we cared for Sarah Castle that feels like laughing tonight!" She tossed her head as though proud of her courage, then singled out Dale for a parting shot. "We're sorry, Mr. Lynch, that you're too good to come with us! Ma, (turning to a meek-faced woman), leave the door unlocked. The meeting'll be a long one."

And just as Mrs. Williams patted down the last sandwich, Mrs. Lynch, with a shaking hand, closed the door and, turning, faced Dale and Robin.

"Well, of all the ungrateful creatures!" cried Beryl, who had taken in the little scene from the kitchen door.

"Now don't you be a-caring, girlie dear," begged Mrs. Lynch, frightened at Robin's stricken face.

Robin turned her glance around the deserted room as though she simply could not believe her eyes. It must surely be an awful dream from which she would awaken. Mrs. Lynch went on, speaking quickly as though to keep back her own tears of disappointment. "It's a grand time the kiddies had this day, bless the little hearts of them, and a loving you like you were some bit of a fairy - the impudence of them -"

"Who are the Rileys?" demanded Robin, sternly - for she *had* to know; the Rileys had spoiled her beautiful plans.

"Now don't you be a-bothering your bright head with the Rileys or anyone else -"

Dale interrupted his mother. On his face still lingered the dark flush that had crept up over it at the black-eyed girl's taunt.

"I don't know why Miss Forsyth *shouldn't* know the reason the Mill people didn't come tonight. There's a big protest meeting about the Rileys - it wasn't gotten up until five o'clock or I'd have told you. Tim Riley's been laid up for six months and he's just back on half-time and can't ever do any better, I guess - and he's been ordered out of his house which means - up the river -"

"Up - where Granny Castle lives?" broke in Robin, in a queer voice.

"Yes. And it's hard on Tim's wife and her children - they're just little things. And he can't go anywhere else, now. It seems Tim's wife went herself to Norris and begged for a little time until she heard from an uncle up in Canada or found some way of earning extra money herself, and Norris wouldn't give in for one day. The men are all pretty sore and they called this meeting -"

"That's where that girl wanted you to go?"

"Yes. And that's why Adam Kraus had to hurry off."

Robin suddenly clutched at her pocket, her face flaming. "Dale, will you hurry - down to that meeting - and take them - this?" She held out a thick roll of bills. "It maybe isn't enough but it will help. I had saved it for something else, but, oh, those babies just *can't* go to that dreadful place -"

Dale shook his head and put his hands behind him.

"That wouldn't go at that meeting, Miss Forsyth. The men would see red. It isn't charity they want - it's justice. They're giving good honest labor to Norris and he isn't fair in return. They're willing to pay to live decently - they just want the chance. And to work decently, too. If you knew the Rileys you'd know what a proud sort they are - they wouldn't take your money any more than I would - or mother, here. If your aunt were home or - if you'd go to Norris -" He considered a moment, frowning. "The men and girls are so roused up that it'll be only a step to organizing and all that sort of thing and these Mills have been pretty free from labor trouble - if only Norris could be made to understand that. But he's so set and out-of-date -" Dale laughed suddenly, a short, bitter laugh, "I suppose I'm extra sore because he refused to even look at my model."

"You all needn't take your spite out on Robin," broke in Beryl, vehemently.

"Well - Miss Robin is a Forsyth and after all that's happened today, the Forsyths aren't very popular with the Mill people. You mustn't blame them too much," turning to Robin. "They're not in the mood to be patronized and they look upon - all this - as a sort of - oh, charity."

Robin looked so bewildered and so small and so distressed that Dale laid his hand comfortingly on her shoulder. His voice rang tender like his mother's. "Don't you be a-worrying your kind little heart! And if you begin right, you'll get your House of Laughter across to them - yet."

"Oh, what do you mean?" Robin caught desperately at the straw he offered.

"Let them pay for it. They can. And they'll be willing to - when they get the idea."

"But I wanted it to be - my gift."

"The opportunity for them to have it *will* be your gift."

Mrs. Lynch suddenly beamed as though she saw a rift in all the clouds.

"Sure, that's the way Miss Lewis talked. And I forgetting it! Let them pay as much as they can and it's a lot more they'll be a-treasuring what's theirs. And no charity about it at all at all! These folks are good, honest folks, dearie, and it's self-respecting they like to feel and a-paying for what they get whether it's the food they eat or a bit of fun. It's a beginning, anyway, this day and you shan't grieve your blessed heart for, if I'm not mistaken, there'll be laughter enough in this house by and by. Mind you what I said once about beginnings had to come first!" Which was a long speech for Mrs. Lynch and amazingly comforting to Robin.

She slipped the roll of bank-notes back into the pocket of her dress; she could not even offer them to Dale, now. "You're dear and patient and I guess I've been stupid and expected too much. But I shan't make any more mistakes and I'm going to make the most of my 'beginning'."

"And now, Dale boy, why not have a bit of Mr. Harkness' good coffee?"

But, though Beryl and Robin pressed, Dale refused and slipped away and Robin had a moment's picture of the triumph of the "horrid" girl when she saw Dale come into the meeting. Then, remembering the plight of the Rileys' she was ashamed of herself for not wanting Dale to go. Sitting around the centre table she and Beryl ate sandwiches while Harkness and Mrs. Lynch and Mrs. Williams sipped coffee. The fire sputtered and gleamed cheerfully, and Sir Galahad's scarlet coat made a brilliant splash of color in the soft glow of the room.

"Who was that big girl with the black eyes?" Robin found the courage to ask Beryl when the whole dreadful evening was over and they were back at the Manor.

"Oh, she's Sophie Mack. She and Sarah Castle were chums and worked together. Dale says she's awfully clever but *I* think she's horrid. The way she spoke to him tonight."

Robin agreed that she was horrid. And she hated to think that her Prince could find this Sophie Mack clever.

Too tired from the disappointing evening to want to talk, and too wide awake to dream of going to sleep, she lay very still until Beryl's deep breathing told her her companion had slipped into dreamland. Then she crept from bed and crouched, a mite of a thing, at the window sill and stared out into the brilliant night. A moon shone coldly over the snowy hills, throwing into bold relief the stacks and buildings of the Mills. Robin recalled that day she had first likened them to a Giant. That day seemed - so much had happened since and she had grown so much inside - very long ago and she a silly girl thinking stories about everything. Her guardian, to amuse her, had talked about finding a Jack to climb the Beanstalk and kill the monster. She smiled scornfully at the fancy - so futile in the face of the tremendous misery - and happiness - that Giant had the power to make!

CHAPTER XVIII

THE LUCKLESS STOCKING

Two hours after Robin's lonely vigil at the window ended, fire destroyed the empty cottage "up the river" into which the Rileys had been ordered to move.

"I wish it had burned in the daytime when we could have watched it," Beryl had declared, almost resentfully. But Robin's concern had been for old Granny Castle and little Susy.

Harkness, who had brought them the news, reassured her. "Too bad they couldn't all a' burned but no such luck - only th' one. It's said that there are some as *knows* how a' empty house without so much as a crumb to draw a rat could a' gone up like that did. And Williams says as how there was men stood around and wouldn't lift a hand to help put out the blaze though they took care it didn't spread."

"What do you mean, Mr. Harkness?" broke in Robin.

"Why, just this, Missy, Williams says that there's a lot of bad feeling stirrin' and bad feelings lead to hasty things like revenge."

"You mean some one of the Mill people set it on fire?" asked Beryl slowly, with wide eyes.

"And who else'd have bad feelings?"

Robin recalled, with alarm, what Dale had said at the House of Laughter. Could Dale have done this thing - or helped? Or stood around and watched it burn? Oh, no, no - not Dale.

Harkness, seeing her concern, dexterously broke a soft-boiled egg into a silver egg-cup and said in a carefully casual voice, intended to put the fire quite out of their minds: "Well, the constable'll find the man what did it, so don't you worry your head, Missy."

Robin, her heart heavy with all she wanted to do and couldn't find a way to do, swallowed a scream at his "Don't you worry your head." Why *did* everyone say that to her - just because she was little on the outside? If *She* didn't worry her head - who was there to worry?

It was with a heavy spirit she dressed herself - girded herself, she called it - for her call upon Mr. Norris at the Mills. The long hours of Sunday, through which she had to wait, had filled her with misgiving. Now she looked so absurdly small in the mirror, her tousled hair so childish, no matter how much she tried to tuck it out of sight under the little dark blue toque, why would anyone, especially a manager of a Mill, listen to her?

Beryl, stirred to sympathy by Robin's daring to face the lion in his den, told her for the hundredth time just how she had suffered before that momentous visit to Martini, the orchestra leader, in New York.

"Why, my hands were clammy and my teeth rattled and everything whirled in front of me and my knees just knocked together, but, say, I gulped and I said terribly hard to myself, 'You want this thing and you can't get it if you're all soft inside and a coward', and, Robin, in a twinkling, something began to grow inside of me and get big and big until I had courage to do anything! Of course it was different with me but you'll probably feel just the way I did, all strong inside, when you face him and get stirred up. Only - I hate to tell you, but I saw you put your stocking on wrong side out and then change it and *that's* bad luck!"

Robin looked down at the luckless stocking. It looked too absurdly a trifle to have weight with anything as important as righting the wrongs of the Rileys.

Afterward, however, Robin vowed she'd always take great care in her dressing!

Frank Norris had been superintendent of the Forsyth Mills for twenty-five years. Since the death of old Christopher Forsyth he had run them pretty much as he pleased, for, inasmuch as his accounting was accurate to the smallest fraction and his profits unfailingly forthcoming, neither Madame Forsyth nor her financial or legal advisers, saw fit to interfere with him. For that reason the old man felt annoyance as well as surprise when Robin broke into the usual routine of his Monday morning, already disturbed by the mystery of Saturday night's fire.

He had duly paid his respects to the little Forsyth heir with a Sunday afternoon call and had afterward reported to Mrs. Norris that she "was a little thing, all red hair and eyes." But now, as she stood at one end of his desk, something in the resolute set of her chin arrested and held his attention; there *was* something more - he could not at the moment say what - to the "little thing" than eyes and red hair.

Robin swallowed (as Beryl had instructed) and plunged straight into her errand. Wouldn't he please let the Rileys stay in their cottage for a little while - until something could be done?

At the mention of the Rileys the smile he had mustered vanished, and his bushy eyebrows drew sharply down over his narrow eyes from which angry little gleams flashed.

"Who asked you to come to me, Miss Forsyth?"

Robin's heart went down into her boots. "No one," she answered in a faint voice. Then, quite suddenly, something in the hard, angry face opposite her fired that spark within her that Beryl had assured her she would feel. She felt the "big thing" grow and grow until she stood straight, quite unafraid, and could go on calmly. "Only I don't think - and I don't believe my aunt would think - it is quite fair to put them out of their house when they've had so much trouble. Hasn't Mr. Riley always been a very good workman? There are lots of things here I don't think quite right, and when my aunt comes back I'm going to ask her to change -"

"May I interrupt you, Miss Forsyth, to inquire upon what experience you base your knowledge? For I assume, of course, you would not want to radically change things here without knowing what you were offering in their place. I was under the impression that you were quite a youngster and had lived with your father in a somewhat Bohemian fashion -"

A deep rose stained Robin's face. She caught the hint of a slur.

"My father taught me what is honest and fair and kind and cruel and -" She had to stop to control the trembling in her voice. The man took advantage of it by breaking in, his voice measured and conciliatory. He suddenly realized the ridiculousness - and the danger - in quarreling with even a fifteen-year-old Forsyth.

"My dear child, I can readily understand in what light certain conditions appear to one of your tender years. When you are older you will understand that an industry such as I am in charge of here, and conducting, I believe, quite satisfactorily for the Forsyths, has to be run by the head and not the heart. I dislike immensely having to do such things as forcing the Rileys to move but you must see it is my duty. If I make an exception in their case - there will be hundreds like them. As it happens -" he let a rasp of anger break into his voice - "the

Jane Abbott

cottage into which they were to move was burned down Saturday night. However that will only delay the enforcing of my order and when the man or men who set fire to it are caught they will be dealt with - severely. Your Rileys will enjoy a few days of grace until we can put another into shape."

"If they burned it it's because they had to show - us - how they felt - that the place wasn't fit to live in! Mr. Norris, the Mill people *are* nice people; I heard - I heard someone say that this was the only Mill in all New England where real white folks worked - but they think we - I mean - the Forsyths - don't care -"

Norris stood up abruptly. Somehow or another he must end this absurd interview while he could yet hang on to his temper. Some one of these miserable agitators - he suspected who it might be - had influenced the girl, was using her for a tool. He had heard, of course, of the intimacy between Miss Gordon and the Lynchs.

"My dear girl - you have no idea how much I would like to go into all this with you and straighten out the muddle in your head - but, really, I am a very busy man. Tell me, didn't young Dale Lynch persuade you to come to me?"

Robin's lips parted impulsively to deny it - then closed. Dale *had* suggested her coming to Norris. Before she could explain, the man went on, a ring of triumph sharpening his voice.

"Ah, I thought so! Now let me tell you why he is disgruntled. I would not look at some contrivance he brought to me which he claims will, when it is perfected, increase the efficiency of our looms fifty per cent. He's a bright young fellow but he doesn't know his place, and he's too chummy with a certain man in these Mills to be healthy for him. However, I'm looking to our friend the town constable to straighten all that out. Now, Miss Gordon," with a hand on her shoulder he gently and in a fatherly manner led her toward the door. "I would suggest, that, without the advice of your aunt - or your guardian - you do not worry your pretty little red head over this!" And he bowed her with pleasant courtesy out of the door.

"Oh! Oh! Oh!" *Another* one telling her not to worry! She clenched her teeth that no one in the outer office might see how near she was to tears. Outside, in a stifled voice, she directed Williams to drive her back to the Manor, then sat very straight in the car as though those hateful eyes could pierce the thick walls and gloat over her defeat.

Halfway to the Manor she remembered suddenly that she had quite ignored the study hours and that doubtless poor Percival Tubbs was pulling his Van Dyke to pieces in his rage. Then in turn she forgot the tutor in a flash of concern for Dale. That beast of a Norris had said something about Dale being too chummy with a certain man - and the constable! Did they suspect Adam Kraus and Dale of setting fire to the cottage? Oh, why had she let him think Dale had suggested her interfering for the Rileys - how stupid she had been! If they arrested Dale and accused him it would be her own fault. A fine way for her to repay dear, dear Mother Lynch. What *could* she do?

Beryl met her with the warning that Mr. Tubbs was "simply furious" - and had said something about "standing this vagary about as long as he could," which did not mean much to Robin, not half so much as Beryl's own ill-temper, for the tutor had taken the annoyance of Robin's high-handed absentedness out on the remaining pupil. With Beryl cross she could not tell her that she had gotten Dale into trouble. She must meet the situation alone.

She must warn Dale, first of all. And to do that she must resort to the distasteful expedient of hanging about in the groceries-and-notions store until Dale passed by after work or stopped for mail as he might possibly do.

She found no difficulty in getting away alone, for Beryl, in the sulks, had buried herself in the deep window-seat of the library. Down in the store she startled the old storekeeper by an almost wholesale order of candies and cookies and topped it off by a demand for a pink knitting wool, which, Robin hoped mightily, might be found only on the topmost shelf. Then, while he was rummaging and grumbling under his breath, she hurriedly told him she *didn't* want it and dropped a crisp five dollar bill on the counter, for the men were pouring down the street and any moment Dale might come.

No coquetting miss, contriving to meet the lad of her fancy, could have planned things to more of a nicety; Robin, her arms full of her absurd purchases, came out of the store just as Dale and Adam Kraus walked along. It was not so much the unusualness of the girl's being there - and alone, that brought Dale to a quick stop; it was the imploring look in her wide and serious eyes.

"Where's Beryl - or that chauffeur?" He took her packages from her.

"I want to talk to you. I *have* to. Will you walk just a little way home with me?"

"Why, what's up? Of course I will. Come, let's cut through here." For Dale realized that many curious eyes were staring at them, and not too kindly. Someone laughed. He would be accused of "truckling" to a Forsyth, which, just then, was likely to bring contempt upon him.

Neither he nor Robin saw the incongruous picture they made; she in her warm suit of softest duvetyn and rich with fur, he in his working clothes, swinging a dinner pail in one hand and in the other balancing her knobby packages. All she thought of was that this was Dale, the Prince who had once befriended her, whose make-believe presence had often gladdened her lonely childhood hours, and who was in danger now; and he looked down into the little face under its fringe of flame-red hair and wondered what in the world made it so tragic and why it strangely haunted him as belonging to some far-off picture in the past.

Vehemently, because it had been bottled up so long, Robin told him how afraid she was for him - that Norris had as much as said he suspected him and Adam Kraus, and that the constable might arrest them any moment and wouldn't he please - go away - or - or something?

"He says you're disgruntled 'cause he wouldn't look at your 'toy.' He's terribly mad about everything - I could see it in his horrid eyes. Oh, I *hate* him!" she finished.

They had left the village and were close to the bend in the road where stood the House of Laughter. Dale stopped short and threw his head back with a loud laugh. Robin had wondered in her heart with what courage her Prince would take the news of his danger but she had not expected this! However, his laugh softened the lines of his face until it looked boyish and oh, so much like it had that night long ago when she had been lost.

"Well, here I am laughing away and forgetting to thank you for wanting to help me. But you needn't be afraid for me, Miss Robin. There is still a little justice in the world, in spite of men like Norris, and I can prove to anyone that I was snug in my bed until my mother dragged me out to go off up to the old village. I can't say I helped fight the fire - what was the use? Nothing could have saved the old place. And I'd rather like to shake hands with the man who set it on fire, though it was sort of a low-down trick. Norris won't house anyone in that rat-hole."

An immense relief shone in Robin's face. She knew Dale had not done the "low-down trick." She wished she had made Norris believe it!

"About the toy -" Dale went on, soberly. "Maybe in the end it'll be a good thing for me that Norris turned it down. Adam Kraus has taken it and he's going to have some little metal contrivances made that it had to have and then he'll take it to Grangers' and he feels pretty sure that Granger will buy it. Only I had a sort of feeling that I wanted it used here - you see these mills gave definite shape to this thing that has been growing in my head for a long time, just like verses in a poet's. I went to a technical night school for years, you know, and I couldn't get enough of the machine shop. One of the teachers in the school got this job for me here. I'd never been outside of New York before and I thought this was Heaven, honest."

"Mr. Norris said you claimed it would - oh, something about efficiency," Robin floundered.

Dale nodded. "I not only claim, I know. That little thing of mine attached to the looms here would revolutionize the whole industry for the Forsyths. You see these Mills are way behind times in their equipment; with improved looms they could turn out more work, pay better wages, and give the men better living and working conditions. And men - the sort they have here - will work better with up-to-date things around them; gives them an up-to-the-minute respect for their job."

Robin stamped her foot in one of her impetuous bursts of anger.

"He ought to be *made* to buy it!" she cried.

Dale turned to her and stared at her intently.

"You're a funny little thing. Why do you care so much?"

Robin had a wild longing to bring back to his mind that November night, long ago, when he had found her clinging abjectly to the palings of the park fence and had taken her home, that she had declared then that he was her play-prince and that she would hunt for him until she found him! And, quite by coincidence, she *had* found him and now she wanted to do this thing for him and not entirely to help the Forsyth Mills! But if she told him - and he laughed - her pretty pretend would be all over and, because it belonged to that happy childhood in the bird-cage with Jimmie, it was precious and she did not want to lose it - yet.

So she flushed and answered shyly: "I - don't - know."

"I'm ever so much obliged, Miss Robin, for your interest and your worry - over me. It gives a fellow a jolly feeling of importance to know that a little girl is bothering her head over his luck. And Miss Robin, you've made things tremendously bright for my mother this winter - and for my father, too. I didn't know whether mother'd be happy here in Wassumsic after being so busy in New York but it was the only way I could stop her from working her head off and I'd decided *my* shoulders were broad enough to support my family. And you've done a lot for Beryl, too. I can see it."

"Oh, *don't!*" cried Robin. As if she could let him thank her for Mother Lynch - as if the debt were not on her side. They had reached the Manor gate now and Dale handed her the packages.

"Everything will come out all right, Miss Robin, so don't you be worrying your little head," he admonished and strangely enough Robin answered him with a smile. *He* was different.

But Robin's "bad" day had not ended yet. Beryl's "sulk" had grown, like the gathering clouds of an impending storm, into a big gloom that did not lighten even when, after dinner, the girls were left alone in the library with their beloved "one thousand and seventy-four" books. From over the edge of "Vanity Fair" Robin watched anxiously the preoccupation and shadow on Beryl's face.

(Oh, why *had* she changed that inside-out stocking!)

"Beryl, what is the matter?"

"Nothing."

"There *is*. You won't read or talk or - anything."

"Well, I don't feel like it."

"What *do* you feel like - inside?" persisted Robin.

"Like - nothing. *Just* like it."

"Beryl, are you discouraged about - your music?"

Robin put her finger so accurately upon the sore spot that Beryl winced. Robin added: "You ought not to be - you're wonderful!"

"I'm *not*. You think so 'cause you don't know! I can't get something I used to have. I had it when I played on Christmas night and oh, I felt as though I'd always have it - it just tingled in my fingers and made my heart almost burst and then - it went away. I can't rouse it now. I don't even know - what made it come - inside me. But I do know that I'm as far away from - what I want, really working and getting ahead - as I ever was. *Further*, way off here. At least when I was in New York I had dear old Jacques Henri to help me!"

Robin's book tumbled to the floor. She had an odd feeling as though Beryl - the first girl friend she had ever had - might be slipping away from her. "You want to go back to New York?" she asked stupidly.

"Of course, silly. There isn't anything, here."

"Then you ought to go. Beryl, you *must* go. I'm going to give you the rest of the money - what I saved from the Queen's Christmas gift and - and - my allowance. Oh, please, Beryl, *don't* look like that!"

"Thanks!" Beryl's voice rang cold. "But I'm not reduced to charity, yet. Of course I've been kidding myself that I earn all the money you pay me for living here - with a few clothes thrown in. Don't think I don't know what those horrid creatures at the Mills say about me being proud and too stuck-up to work like Dale and the others. They even taunt Dale. I hate myself when I think of it. And all I'm earning wouldn't keep me very long - if I ever did go to study. Oh, I just hate - *hate - hate* being poor!" Her voice broke in a great sob.

Robin wanted to throw her arms about her and comfort her but she was afraid for Beryl looked like a different being. And, while she hesitated, Beryl flung herself out of the room.

Robin stared into the fire, little lines of worry and perplexity wrinkling her face. Everything was so stupidly hard; no matter what she tried or wanted to do - she ran up against a wall of pride. Her poor little treasured money that she had kept in the heart-shaped box! If she had had it in her hands then she would have thrown it into the fire.

Oh, for a chance to do something, give something that could not be counted - and spurned - in dollars and cents!

Jane Abbott

CHAPTER XIX

GRANNY

Thoroughly exhausted by the nervous strain of the day before Robin slept late. When she awakened it was to the alarming realization that Beryl was not with her - her bed was empty, the room deserted, from the bathroom came no sound of splashing water, with which Beryl usually emphasized her morning dip.

The unhappy happenings of the evening just past flashed into Robin's mind. Beryl had not even said good-night, had pretended to be asleep. What if she had gone away from the Manor?

The thought was so upsetting that Robin dressed in frantic haste, paying careful regard to her stockings, however, and tumbled down the stairs, almost upsetting Harkness and a tray of breakfast.

"Where's Beryl?" she demanded.

"Miss Beryl's gone, Missy. She got up early and went off directly she had breakfast."

"Did she - did she have a bag?" faltered poor Robin.

"Why, yes, Missy, she had that bag she come with 'near as I can remember. Didn't she tell you she was going?"

"Well - not so early," Robin defended.

"If it's a quarrel, and young people fall out more times 'n not, Missy, don't you feel badly. Miss Beryl'll be back here, mark my words! She's smart enough to know when things are soft."

"Don't you ever, *ever* say that again, Harkness! Beryl didn't want to stay here in the first place. She's proud and she's fine and she had ambitions that are grander than anything the rest of us ever dreamed of. It's just because it *is* soft here that she didn't want to stay. She thought she wasn't really earning anything. I should think -" and oh, how her voice flayed poor trembling Harkness, "I should think if you *cared* anything about me you'd be dreadfully sorry to have me left alone here -"

"Now, Missy! Miss Robin! Old Harkness'll go straight down to the village and bring Miss Beryl -"

Robin laid her hand on the old man's arm. "I just said that to punish you. No, I'll be very lonesome here but I will *not* send for Beryl. We'll get along someway. If I only were not rich, everything would go all right, wouldn't it, Mr. Harkness?"

"Well, I don't just get your meaning but I will. And I guess so, Missy. And now what do you say to a bite of breakfast - fetched hot from the kitchen to your own sunny room?"

Robin knew she would break the old man's heart if she refused his service so she climbed back up the stairs to the sunny window of the deserted sitting-room and awaited the tray of hot breakfast. And as she sat there her eyes suddenly fell upon Cynthia, sitting straight among the cushions of the chaise longue, staring at her with faded, unblinking eyes. Beryl had not taken the doll!

A great hurt pressed hard against Robin's throat. Beryl had *wanted* to make her feel badly. But why - oh, what had she done?

"You can stay there, Cynthia. *I* won't touch you," she cried, turning to the window, and at the same time she registered the vow in her heart that by no littlest word or act of hers should Beryl know how her desertion had hurt her.

A week of stormy weather, which made the roads almost impassable, helped Robin. She threw herself into her studies with a determination almost as upsetting to Percival Tubbs as her former indifference. And when the studies were over she buried herself in the great divan before the library fire with books piled about her while Harkness hovered near at hand, watching her with an anxious eye.

Robin did not always read the open page. Sometimes, holding it before her, she let her mind go over word by word what Dale had said to her as they walked home from the store. It had not been much, to be sure, but it had been enough to make her feel that her Prince had opened his heart to her, oh, just a tiny bit. With her blessed powers of imagination and with what Beryl had told her from time to time concerning him, she could put everything together into a beautiful picture.

Dale was splendid and brave - *He* had not been afraid of being poor! And he dreamed, too, like Sir Galahad, but a dream of machinery. And he had had a beautiful light in his face when he had said that about his shoulders being broad enough to support his family. Oh, Robin wished she could see him in a scarlet coat like Sir Galahad wore in the picture.

The snowstorm abating, Robin sent Williams to the village with a basket of flowers for Mrs. Lynch and fruit for big Danny, and Williams brought back a tenderly grateful little note from Mrs. Lynch - but not a word from Beryl.

"Everything must be all right or she'd have told me," Robin assured herself. "Anyway Mr. Norris would be *afraid* to arrest anyone like Dale."

What Robin did *not* know - for it was not likely to disturb the

Manor - was that something far crueller than Norris was claiming the anxiety of the Mill workers. A malignant epidemic had lifted its ugly head and had crept stealthily into several homes, claiming its victims in more than one. Norris feared an epidemic more than labor trouble; unless it could be quickly stamped out it gave the Mills a bad name and made it difficult to get hands. So, at its first appearance he called the Mill doctor into consultation, and urged him to do everything in his power to check the advance of the disease.

The Mill doctor, an overworked man, wanted to tell Norris that it was a pity that the whole "old village" had not gone up in smoke, but he refrained from doing so; instead spoke optimistically of the weather being in their favor, and went away.

On an afternoon three weeks after Beryl's sudden and inexplainable departure, the drowsy quiet of the old Manor was broken by a shrill voice lifted in frenzied protest against Harkness' deeper tones. It brought Percival Tubbs from his nap, Mrs. Budge from the pantry and Robin from the library. There in the hall stood poor little Susy, her old cap pushed back from her flaming cheeks, her eyes dark with fright, struggling to escape from Harkness' tight hold.

At sight of Robin her voice broke into a strangling sob.

"Oh! Oh! *Oh!*"

"She won't tell me her errand," explained Harkness, looking like a guilty schoolboy caught in a bully's act.

"Harkness, shame on you! Let her go," cried Robin.

Freed from Harkness' hold Susy ran to Robin and clasped her knees. She was shaking so violently that she could do nothing more than make funny, incoherent sounds which were lost in the folds of Robin's skirt.

"See how you've frightened her! Susy-girl, don't. *don't.* You're with the big girl. Tell me, what is the matter?"

Suddenly Susy pulled at Robin's hand and, still sobbing, dragged her resolutely toward the door. Robin caught something about "Granny."

"Something dreadful must have happened to frighten her," Robin declared to the others. "Won't you tell Robin, Susy? Do you want Robin to go with you to Granny's?"

At this Susy nodded violently, but when Robin moved to get her wraps she burst forth in renewed wailing and clung tightly to Robin's hand.

"Harkness, please get my coat and hat and overshoes. I'm going back with Susy. Something's happened -"

"Miss Gordon, indeed, you better not -" implored Harkness.

"Hurry! Haven't you tormented the poor child enough? Don't stand there like wood. If you don't get my things *at once* I'll go bareheaded!"

Harkness went off muttering and Percival Tubbs advanced a protest which Robin did not even hear, so concerned was she in soothing poor Susy.

In a few moments she was hurrying down the winding drive which led to the village, with difficulty keeping up with Susy, leaving behind in the great hall of the Manor an annoyed tutor, a worried butler and an outraged housekeeper.

More than one on the village street turned to stare at the strange little couple, Susy, pale with fright, two spots of angry red burning her cheeks, running as though possessed, and Robin limping after her with amazing speed and utterly indifferent to anyone she met.

As they neared the old village Susy's pace suddenly slowed down and Robin took advantage of that to ask her more concerning Granny.

"Granny's queer and all cold and she won't speak to me, she won't!" Susy managed to impart between gasps.

A terrible fear gripped Robin. Perhaps Granny was dead! And her apprehension was confirmed when a neighbor of the Castles rushed out to head her off.

"Don't go in there! Don't go in there!" she cried, waving the shawl she had caught up to wrap around her head. "They've got the sickness. The old woman's dead. Tommy's staying at Welch's. My man's reportin' it this mornin'. Poor old woman, went off easy, I guess, but it's hard on the kid. Say, Miss, you oughtn' get close to her. It's awful catchin' and you c'n tell by the look o' her she's got it, too." And the neighbor edged away from Susy.

In a sort of stupefied horror Robin looked at the neighbor, the wretched house and Susy. Susy had begun to cry again, quietly, and to tremble violently.

"Susy Castle, you go like a good girl into the house n' stay 'til the doctor comes and takes you," commanded the woman. "Don' you come near anyone! Y' got the sickness! See y' shake!"

"Go 'way!" screamed Susy, clinging to Robin. Robin pulled her fur from her throat and wrapped it about the shivering, sobbing child.

"Yer takin' awful chances, miss - just *awful*," warned the neighbor, edging backward toward her house with the air of having completed her duty. "If y' take my advice you'll leave the kid there 'til some'un comes. They'll likely take her t' the poor-house!" And with this cheerful assumption she slammed her door.

"There! There! Robin'll take you home. Don't cry," begged Robin, kneeling in the path and encircling poor little Susy in her arms. "We'll go back to the big house and Robin'll make you nice and warm."

"I want Granny!" wailed the child, feeling her miserable little world rocking about her.

Robin straightened and looked at the house. Granny was dead, the neighbor had said; nothing more could be done for her. But something in the desolation of the place, the boarded door, the dingy window stuffed with its rags, smote Robin. Poor Granny must have died all alone. No one had even whispered a good-bye. And she lay in there all alone. Robin knew little of death; to her it had always meant a beautiful passing to somewhere, with lovely flowers and music and gentle grief. This was horribly different - there was no one left but little Susy and she was going to take Susy away at once. Ought she not to just go softly into that house and do *something* - something kind and courteous that Granny, somewhere above, might see - and like?

"Wait here, Susy. I'll be back in a moment." She walked resolutely around to the door which Susy, in her flight, had left half-open. At the threshold a cold dread seized her, sending shivers racing down her spine, catching her breath, bringing out tiny beads of moisture on her forehead. She had never seen a dead person - had she the courage?

She tiptoed softly into the room, her eyes staring straight ahead. In its centre she stopped and looked slowly, slowly around as though dragging her gaze to the object she dreaded - across the littered table, the cupboard, the stove crowded with unwashed pots and pans, the dirty floor, an overturned chair, the smoke-blackened lamp and last - last to the bed. There, amid the tumbled quilts, lay poor Granny.

Robin swallowed what she knew was her heart and walked to the bed. "Granny," she said softly, because she had to say something, then almost screamed in terror at the sound of her own voice. Strangely enough there was a smile on the worn, thin lips. In her high-strung condition Robin thought it had just come - she liked to *think* it had just come. It gave her courage. She smoothed the dirty gray covers and folded them neatly across the still form, careful not to touch the withered hands. Then she looked about. Her eyes lit on the faded pink flowers that still adorned the what-not. Moving with frightened speed she caught them up and carefully laid them on Granny's breast.

"They were beautiful once and so was poor Granny. Goodbye, Granny," she whispered, moving backward toward the door. Out in the air she leaned for a moment weakly against the door jamb - then resolutely pulled herself together, and carefully closed the door behind her.

Susy stood where she had left her. "Come, Susy, let's hurry," Robin cried. Catching the child's hand she broke into a run, wondering if she could get back to the Manor before that dreadful sickening thing inside of her quite overcame her.

But at that moment Williams appeared in the automobile, jumped from the seat and caught Robin just as she started to drop in a little heap to the ground.

"Miss Robin!" he cried in alarm.

The feel of his strong arms and the warmth and shelter of his great coat sent the life surging back through Robin's veins. She laughed hysterically.

"Take us home, quick," she implored. And so concerned was Williams that he made no protest at lifting Susy into the car.

Both Harkness and Mrs. Budge, with different feelings, were waiting Williams' return in the hall of the Manor. Harkness, with real concern, (he had despatched Williams) and Mrs. Budge with defiance. She had just announced that she'd stood about as much as any woman "who'd give her whole life to the Forsyths ought t' be expected to stand" when Robin half-carried Susy into the Manor.

"Harkness, *please* - Susy's very ill. Will you carry her to my room and call the doctor?"

"You'll do no such thing while *I* stay in this house," announced Mrs. Budge, stepping forward and placing her bulk between Harkness and Susy. "Bringing this fever what's in the village to *This* house! Not if my name's Hannah Budge. We've had just 'bout as much of these common carryings-on as I'll stand for with Madame away and -"

"But, oh, *please*, Mrs. Budge, Susy's very sick and her grandmother's just died and she's all alone! Harkness, *won't* you?"

"Oh, Missy, I think Budge -" began Harkness, his eyes imploring.

Robin stamped her foot.

"Shame on you all! You're just *afraid*. Will you call a doctor at least - one of you? Get out of my way!" And half carrying - half dragging Susy, Robin staggered to the stairs and slowly up them.

Poor Robin vaguely remembered Jimmie once commanding Mrs. Ferrari to put one of her brood into a tub of hot water into which he mixed mustard. So Robin filled her gleaming tub with hot water and quickly undressed Susy and put her, wailing, into it. Then she rushed to the pantry, commandeered a yellow box, fled back and dropped a generous portion of its contents into the tub. Next she spread a soft woolly blanket on her bed, wrapped another around the child and rolled her in both until nothing but the tip of a pink nose showed.

She found Harkness hovering outside in the hall and ordered

him to bring hot lemonade at once, taking it a few minutes later from him through the half-open door with a gleam of contempt in her eyes which said plainly "Coward." She slowly fed Susy, watching the child's face anxiously and wishing the doctor would come quickly.

After an interminable time Dr. Brown came, a little shaky, and gray-eyed and very concerned over his call to the Manor. After a careful examination he reported to Percival Tubbs and Harkness that the child was, indeed, desperately ill; that by no means could she be moved - although it was of course a pity that Miss Forsyth had so impulsively brought her to the Manor and thus exposed herself; that the crisis might come within the next twenty-four hours, for evidently the disease was well advanced before the grandmother succumbed; that he would telegraph at once for a fresh nurse from New York as the one in the village was at the breaking point from overwork; and that he, himself, would come back and stay with the child through the night.

It was a most dreadful night for everyone in the Manor - except Percival Tubbs, who had slipped quietly to the station and taken the evening train to New York. Harkness sat outside of Robin's door, his ear strained for the slightest sound within. And Mrs. Budge worked far into the night writing a letter to Cornelius Allendyce, commanding that gentleman to come to the Manor and see for himself how things were going and put an end, once and for all, to the whole nonsense - that she'd up and walk out if it weren't for her loyalty to Madame Forsyth, a loyalty sadly strained in the last few months. Of course she did not write all this in just these same words but she made her meaning very clear.

Behind the closed door Dr. Brown and Robin fought for the little life. Only once the tired doctor said more than a few words - then it was to tell Robin that she had shown remarkable judgment in her care of Susy and that - if the child pulled through - it would be due entirely to her prompt and thorough action. This little thought helped Robin through the long hours, when her weary eyelids stuck over her hot, dry eyes and her head ached. All night she willingly fetched and carried at the doctor's command, stepping noiselessly, sometimes lingering at the foot of the bed to watch the little face for a sign of change.

Far into the morning the vigil lasted. Then Dr. Brown, his face haggard but his eyes shining, whispered to Robin to go off downstairs and eat a good breakfast - that Susy was "better."

"You mean - she'll - get well?"

The doctor nodded. "I believe so. She's sleeping now. Go, my dear."

Robin peeped at the child's face. The deadly pallor and the purple flush of fever had gone, the lips and eyelids had relaxed into the natural repose of sleep. She tiptoed into the hall, deserted for the moment, down the stairs, and into the kitchen. Mrs. Budge turned as she pushed open the door.

"I - I -" The warm, sweet smell of the room sent everything dancing before Robin's eyes. She reached out her hand as though groping for support. "Oh, I -" Then she crumpled into Mrs. Budge's arms.

Now that faithful soul, having sent off her letter to the lawyer-man, had given herself over to worry, lest once more the "curse" was to visit the House of Forsyth. Not that it could mean much to Madame, for she hadn't set eyes on this girl Gordon, but it gave her, Hannah Budge, a sick feeling "at the pit of her stomach" to think of things going wrong again! So when Robin just dropped into her arms like a dead little thing she stood as one stunned, passively awaiting a relentless Fate.

"Quick - she's fainted. Let me take her! Fetch water," ordered Harkness.

"Fetch it yourself! I guess I can hold her!" retorted Budge, tightening her clasp. And as she looked down at Robin she remembered how Robin had kissed her on Christmas night. Something within her that was hard like rock commenced to soften and soften and grow warm and glow all through her. Her eyes filled with tears and because both hands were occupied and she could not wipe them away, she shook her head and two bright drops rolled down her cheeks into Robin's face. At that moment - even before Harkness brought his water - Robin stirred and opened her eyes and smiled.

"Oh - where am I? Oh - yes. Oh, I'm *so* hungry!"

But Budge was certain Robin was desperately ill; under her direction Harkness carried her to Madame's own room while Mrs. Budge followed with blankets and a hot water bottle. At noon the nurse arrived from New York, and that evening the word spread to every corner of Wassumsic that little Miss Forsyth had the "sickness."

CHAPTER XX

ROBIN'S BEGINNING

Robin had done something that couldn't be counted - or spurned - in dollars and cents.

From door to door in the village the story spread; how Robin had gone into the stricken cottage which even the neighbors shunned, and had performed a last little act (and the only one) of respect for poor old Granny, then, with her own fur around the child's neck, had taken Susy back to the Manor. The doctor told of Robin's sensible care and how ably she had shared with him the night's long vigil. The story was told and re-told with little embellishments and often tears; the girls in the Mill repeated each detail of it over their lunches, the men talked about it in low tones as they walked homeward.

And Robin's little service had a remarkable effect upon the Mill people. Tongues that had been most bitter against the House of Forsyth suddenly wagged loudest in Robin's praise; some boldly foretold the beginning of a "better day." All felt the stirring of a certain, all-promising belief that a Forsyth, even though a small one - "cared."

But what was to be the cost, they asked one another, with anxious faces?

Upon hearing that Robin herself was ill, Beryl had rushed to the Manor, in an agony of fear. Robin mustn't be sick - she couldn't die! It was too dreadful - She ought never to have gone into Granny Castle's house - or touched Susy.

Among the books Robin loved so well Beryl waited in a dumb misery for hours, for some word. Harkness only shook his old head at her and Mrs. Budge ignored her. Finally, standing the suspense as long as she could she crept to the stairs and up them and in the hall above encountered a cherry-faced white-garbed young woman.

"May I see Robin, please?" she implored desperately.

The young woman looked at her, hesitating. "Are you Beryl?" she asked. Beryl nodded. "Then you may go in for a few moments but don't let that old man and woman know - they've been hounding me to let them see her and I've refused flatly."

"Oh, thank you so much. There's something I have to tell Robin before -" Beryl simply could not say it. She closed her lips with tragic meaning.

The nurse stared at her a moment with a hint of a laugh in her eyes, then nodded toward the door.

"Second door, there. Only a minute!" And then she went on.

Beryl opened the door, softly, her heart pounding against her ribs. What if Robin were too ill to talk, to even listen -

Beryl had never seen Madame's bed room. It took a moment for her to single out the great canopied bed from the other mammoth furnishings - or to take in the small figure that occupied the exact centre of that bed.

"Beryl!" came a glad cry and Beryl stared in amazement for the little creature who smiled at her from a pile of soft pillows looked like anything but a sick person; the vivid hair glowed with more aliveness than ever, a pink, like the inner heart of a rose, tinted the creamy skin. A tray remained on a low table by the bed, its piled dishes indicative of a feast. Beryl's amazed eyes flashed last to these then back to Robin's smiling face.

"Oh, Beryl, I'm so glad, *glad* you came!" Robin reached out her arms and Beryl rushed into them, clasping her own close about Robin.

"I - I thought you were dreadfully sick," she gasped, at last. She drew back and looked at Robin accusingly. "*Everyone* thinks you're dreadfully sick."

"Then I suppose I ought to be," laughed Robin, "I'm not, though, I never felt better in my life. But, oh, right after I knew Susy would get well everything inside of me seemed to break into little pieces. Then that nice Miss Sanford came and put me to bed and nursed and petted and fed me and - here I am. She says I cannot get up until tomorrow. I'm so anxious to see Susy!"

Beryl, still holding Robin's hand, stared off into space, uncomfortably. She had come to the Manor to tell Robin (before Robin should die) that she had been a mean, selfish, ungrateful thing to run away from the Manor the way she had done and stay away - and to beg for Robin's forgiveness. Now she found it difficult to say all this to a pinky, glowing Robin, and Robin, instinctively guessing what was passing in Beryl's mind, made her plea for forgiveness unnecessary by asking, with a tight squeeze of Beryl's hand: "You won't go away, again?"

"No - at least - if you want me - if -" she stumbled.

"*If* I want you - Beryl Lynch! It was too dreadful living here all alone with only Mr. Tubbs and Harkness and Mrs. Budge. But, Beryl, I think maybe everything will be different now; the first thing I knew after I fainted was that Mrs. Budge was crying! Think of it, Beryl, *crying* - and over me! And Mr. Tubbs ran away."

"Really, truly?"

"Yes - the poor thing was scared silly. He didn't tell a soul he was going and after he reached New York he telephoned."

"Dale says everyone at the Mills is talking about you, Robin - and what you did."

"Why," Robin's face sobered, "I didn't do - anything."

"Well, Dale says your going in to poor old Granny the way you did has made everyone like you. And they were getting awfully worked up against the Forsyths and the Mills. I will admit it seems funny to me - making such a fuss over such a little thing. I wish - as long as you're all right now - you had done something real heroic, like jumping into the river to save someone or going into a burning building."

"Oh, I'd have never had the courage to do *that*," protested Robin, shuddering.

At that moment the nurse put her head in the door.

"Three minutes are up," she warned.

"Please, can't she stay?" begged Robin, in alarm.

"I must go home, anyway, Robin, to tell mother. You have no idea how anxious she is - everyone is. People hang around our door. I suppose they think we have the latest news about you. Well, we have, now. And, Robin - mother was awfully angry about my - leaving you the way I did. She begged me to come back, long ago. I'm sorry, now, I didn't. Good-bye, Robin. I'll be back, tomorrow."

Beryl walked to the village in a deep absorption of thought. Certain values she had fostered had tumbled about and had to be put in order. Here were not only hundreds of mill folk making a "fuss" over what Robin had done, but the household of the Manor as well - old Budge, usually as adamant as a brick wall, crying! No one loved the heroic more than Beryl, but to her thinking it lay in a spectacular, and with a dramatic indifference, risking one's own life for another, not in a little unnecessary sentimental impulse. When she had heard of what Robin had done she had declared her "crazy" to go near the Castles, to which her mother had indignantly replied: "And are you thinking the blessed child ever thinks of herself at all?" *that* was the quality, of course, about Robin that you never guessed from anything she said but that you just felt. And the Mill people were feeling it now.

Turning these thoughts over and over, Beryl suddenly faced the disturbing conviction that she was moulding her own young life on very opposite lines. Tell herself as often as she liked - and it was often - that she'd had to fight to get everything she had and to keep it, she knew that it never crossed her mind to ask herself what she was giving - to Dale, who carried a double burden, to poor big Danny, to her brave little mother who had sheltered her so valiantly from the coarsening things about her that she might keep "fine" and have "fine" things.

The next day the nurse let Robin dress, to poor Harkness' tearful delight. And Robin, roaming the house as though she had returned to it from a long absence, found, indeed, the change she had prophesied. For Mrs. Budge, in strangely genial mood, was fussily preparing more delectable invalid dishes than a dozen convalescing Susies or well Robins could possibly eat.

One little cloud, however, shadowed Budge's relief. She wished she hadn't sent the letter to the lawyer-man. "If I'd remembered how my grandmother always said to look out for the written word, and held my tongue," she mourned and so complete was her transformation that she forgot she had written that letter while in full pursuit of her duty to the Forsyths - as she had seen it then.

Upon this new order of things Cornelius Allendyce arrived, unheralded, and very tired from a long journey. Budge's letter had been forwarded to him at Miami where he had been pleasantly recuperating from his siege of sciatica. It had disturbed him tremendously, and he had spent the long hours on the railroad train upbraiding himself for his neglect of his ward. The conditions at which Budge had clumsily hinted grew more serious as he thought of them, until he found himself wondering if perhaps he ought not to smuggle his little ward back to her fifth-floor home before Madame discovered the havoc she had made of the Forsyth traditions.

Outwardly, the Manor appeared the same, to the lawyer's intense relief. Within, the most startling change seemed the laughing voices that floated out to him from the library. Harkness took his coat and hat and bag a little excitedly and with repeated nods toward the library.

"Miss Robin'll be mighty glad to see you, I'm sure; but she has a lydy guest for dinner."

"The man actually acts as though I had no right to come unannounced," thought Cornelius Allendyce.

Robin met him with a rush and a glad little cry. "I thought you were never, *never* coming! I'm so glad. But why didn't you send us word? I want you to know Beryl's mother and Beryl. They're my best friends. And, oh, I have *so* much to tell you!"

"Mrs. Lynch!" A line of Budge's letter flashed across the man's mind, yet he found himself talking to a gentle-faced woman with grave eyes and a tender, merry mouth. And Beryl (whom Budge had called "that young person") did not seem at all coarse or unwholesome. He did not notice that the clothes both wore were simple and inexpensive - he only registered the impression that the mother seemed quiet and refined and the girl had a frank honesty in her face that was most pleasing.

Robin, indeed, had so much to tell him that he made no effort to get "head or tail" to it; rather he lost himself in wonder at the change in his little ward. This spirited, assured young person could not be the same little thing he had left months ago. She'd actually grown, too.

He laughed at Robin's description of the desertion of Percival Tubbs.

"Poor man, I guess I'd driven him crazy, anyway. I simply couldn't learn the lessons he gave me. But, oh, I haven't wasted my time, truly, for I've gotten more out of these precious books here than I ever got out of school. Guardian dear, *they've* made me grow. I don't think my pretend stories any more, either. I can't seem to, for everything about me is so real and so big and so - so important." Robin imparted this information with a serious note in her voice - as though she feared her guardian might be sorry that she had put her childish "pretends" behind her.

"Dear me," he said, "then we won't know whether you meet the Prince in the last chapter and live happily ever after? You *have* grown up; I can't get used to it."

Robin blushed furiously at this and changed the subject lest her guardian could glimpse under her flaming hair and guess the one pretty "pretend" she still cherished.

While the girls were upstairs Mrs. Lynch told Cornelius Allendyce the story of Susy, and Robin's visit to the old house. She told it simply but in its every detail so that Robin's guardian could follow it very closely. He listened, with his eyes dropped to the rug at his feet, and for a few moments he kept them there, so that Mrs. Lynch wondered if he were angry. Then suddenly he looked at her and a smile broke over his face.

"Our little girl's letting down a few barriers, isn't she?" he asked, and Mrs. Lynch, understanding him with her quick instinct, nodded with bright eyes.

"Ah, 'tis true as true what my old Father Murphy once said to me - that wealth is what you give, not what you get!"

The most amazing thing to the lawyer in the new order was the cheerful importance, and the new geniality of Hannah Budge. Accustomed as he was, from long acquaintance with the family, to her sour nature, he caught himself watching her now in a sort of unbelief. He understood her attentiveness to his comfort when she touched his arm and begged a word with him.

"It's about that letter," she whispered, her eyes rolling around for any possible eavesdropper. "I'll ask you not to tell Miss Gordon nor Timothy Harkness. I'm old and new ways are new ways but I'll serve Miss Gordon as I've always served the Forsyths."

A dignity in the old housekeeper's surrender touched Cornelius Allendyce. He patted her shoulder and told her not to worry about the letter; to be sure it had spoiled a rather nice golf match but he ought to have run up to Wassumsic long before.

"The little girl I found isn't such a bad Forsyth, after all?" he could not resist asking her, however. But Harkness, appearing at that moment, spared Mrs. Budge the unaccustomed humiliation of admitting she had been wrong.

After dinner Robin persuaded her guardian to walk with them to the village while they escorted "Mother Lynch" home, and then stop at the House of Laughter. There, Beryl lighted the lamps and Robin led a tour of inspection through the rooms, telling her guardian as they went, of her beautiful plans and their failure. At a warning sign from Beryl she regretfully left out the generous contribution of their mysterious Queen of Altruria. Most of the furniture, she explained, had come from the Manor garrets.

While they were talking a knock sounded at the door. Robin

opened it to find Sophie Mack and three companions standing on the threshold.

"Mrs. Lynch said she thought you were up here," Sophie explained, awkwardly. "We're getting up a social club and we want to know if you'll let us meet here."

"Of course you can meet here!" Robin made no effort to control the surprise in her voice. "That's what this little house is for."

"Maybe you'll join, sometime. As an honorary member or something like that -" one of Sophie's companions broke in.

"Oh, I'd love to."

"We want to pay, you know," persisted Sophie.

"Of course - anything you - think you can."

The girls, refusing Robin's invitation to go into the cottage, turned and went back to the village. Robin closed the door and leaned against it with a long-drawn breath of delight.

"Guardian dear, *that's* the beginning. Dale's right - they'll use it, if I let them pay. Why are you laughing at me?"

Cornelius Allendyce's face sobered. He drew the girl to him.

"I'm not laughing. I'm only marvelling at the leaps and bounds with which your education has gone forward. Some people die at an old age without acquiring one smallest part of the human understanding you are learning through these - notions - of yours."

Robin made a little face. "Notions! Beryl calls them 'crazy ideas.' *Someone else* called them an 'experiment.' Dear Mother Lynch is the *only* one who really believes in what I want to do. You see, I just want the people here to think that a Forsyth cares whether they're happy or not. Dale says I didn't start right and maybe I didn't - but anyway -" - She nodded toward the door as though Sophie might still be on the threshold, "*they're* a beginning!"

Her guardian did not answer this and looked so strange that Robin went no further in her confidences. Perhaps something had displeased him, she must wait until some other time to tell him about Dale and his model and her visit to Frank Norris.

Back in the library, before the crackling fire, Robin begged Beryl to play for her guardian.

"She's wonderful," she whispered while Beryl was getting the violin. "She makes you feel all funny inside."

Beryl stood in the shadow and played. Robin, watching her guardian, thrilled with satisfaction when the man's face betrayed that he, too, felt "all funny inside" under the magic of Beryl's bow.

"Come here, my girl," he commanded when Beryl stopped. He bent a searching look upon her. "Come here and sit down and tell me about yourself."

"Didn't I say she's wonderful?" chirped Robin, triumphantly.

The lawyer's adroit questioning brought out Beryl's story - of the simple home in the tenement from which her mother shut out all that was coarsening and degrading, stirring her child's mind and her tastes with dreams she persistently cherished against disheartening odds; of the Belgian musician who had first taught her small fingers and fired her ambitions for only the best in the art; of school and the lessons she devoured because she craved knowledge and the advantages of possessing it.

"How long have you lived here?"

"We came last summer. Dale wanted to work where there were machines and he got a job in the Forsyth Mills."

"You are planning to go back to New York and study?"

Beryl's face clouded. "Sometime. But I can't until I earn the money, and it takes such a lot."

"Yes, and courage, too," added the lawyer softly, as though he were speaking to himself.

Beryl abruptly lifted her violin from her lap to put it in the case. As she did so, its head caught in the string of green beads which, in honor of the occasion, she was wearing. The slender cord that held them snapped and the pretty beads scattered over the floor.

"Oh, dear!" cried Beryl, dismayed, dropping to her knees to find them.

Robin helped her search and in a few moments they had gathered them all.

"They're only beads but they're very old and a keepsake," Beryl explained, in apology for her moment's alarm.

"They're pretty and they're darling on you!"

"A wonderful color." The lawyer took one and examined it. "If you care for them you'd better let me take them back to New York with me and have them strung on a wire that will not break."

"Oh, let him, Beryl. And he can have a good clasp put on. You know you said that clasp was poor."

Beryl hesitated a moment. Ought she to tell him the beads were her mother's and that her mother prized them dearly? No, he might laugh at anyone's caring a fig about just plain beads. She took the envelope Robin brought her, dropped the beads into it, sealed it, and gave it to Robin's guardian.

Cornelius Allendyce slept little that night. He laid it to the extreme quiet of the hills; in reality his head whirled with the amazing impressions that had been forced upon him.

"Extraordinary!" he muttered, staring at the night light. And he repeated it again and again; once, when he thought of the little woman, Mrs. Lynch, with the dreaming eyes which seemed to see beyond things. What was the absurd thing she had said? "'Tis what you give and not what you get is wealth." Extraordinary! And where had Robin picked up these notions concerning the Mill people? And her House of What-did-she-call-it? There was considerable significance about it. Uncanny, downright uncanny, though, for a girl her age to have such a far-reaching vision. Probably the child didn't realize, herself. Well, there was Jeanne d'Arc, and others, too, he pondered, hazily. And this talented girl Robin had found - a most unusual girl, who'd grown up in a tenement like a flower among weeds, yes, he'd seen such flowers growing amid rankest vegetation! She was not unlike Robin, herself. His mind circled to Robin's own little fifth-floor nest and the horrible odors of that dark stairway. Strange, extraordinary, that these two lives had crossed. "This world's a queer world!" Both girls brought up in a poverty that denied them all those jolly sort of advantages young girls liked, and yet each sheltered by a mother's great love from the things in poverty that coarsen and hurt. "Aye, a mother's love," and the little lawyer thought of "Mother Lynch" with something very akin to reverence; and of Jimmie, too, poor Jimmie, who, in his stumbling, mistaken way, had tried to give a mother's love to Robin.

But suddenly the man aroused from his absorbed philoso-phizing and sat bolt upright in bed. All right to think about letting down barriers - whose barriers were they? Proud old Madame loved those barriers - and she'd never accept, as Budge had, what Budge called the "new ways." What then?

"There'll be a reckoning -"

With a sharp little exclamation of annoyance the distraught guardian drew his watch from under his pillow and held it to the tiny shaft of light. "Half-past-one!" Well, he did not need to cross that bridge until he came to it! He dug his tired head into his pillow and went to sleep to dream of Madame Forsyth and Robin and Jeanne d'Arc sitting in a social club at the House of Laughter.

CHAPTER XXI

AT THE GRANGER MILLS

"I really think, little Miss Robin, that you ought to go."

"Why, I should think you'd be *crazy* to go!"

"If I may be so bold's to remind you, the man is waiting for an answer."

Robin looked from her guardian's face to Beryl's to Harkness'.

"You're all conspiring against me, I do believe!" she cried. "I'll go if you say I ought to, but I just hate to. I don't want to meet the young people, there. And I'm dreadfully afraid of Mrs. Granger since Susy spoiled her dress."

"Mrs. Granger was one of your Aunt Mathilde's closest friends - until the death of young Christopher. Then, in the strange mood your aunt encouraged, she let the intimacy drop. I've often wondered if the Grangers did not resent that. You have an opportunity now, Robin, to restore the old terms between the two families, so that when your - aunt returns she will find the old tie awaiting her."

Robin stared, wide-eyed, at her guardian. It was the first time he had spoken of her aunt's return.

"When is my aunt coming back? Do you know I never *think* of her coming back? Isn't that dreadful? I know she won't like me -"

"Don't let's worry about that now," broke in Cornelius Allendyce with suspicious haste. And Harkness, standing stiffly by the table, waiting instructions, fell suddenly to rearranging the books and magazines which had been in perfect order.

Mrs. Granger's chauffeur had brought a note to the Manor asking Robin to make them a few days' visit during the coming week. "My son and daughter have some young people here and you will find it a lively change from the quiet of your aunt's."

Robin used her last argument. "But you've only been here for a few days, guardian dear. And there's a *lot* more I want to tell you - oh, that's very important."

"Can't it wait until I come again? I'd have to go back to New York tomorrow, my dear, anyway. Come, this little visit of yours is as necessary to your education as a Forsyth as any of Mr. Tubbs' tiresome lessons. And then, as I said, you can win back my lady Granger's affection."

"Well, I'll go," cried Robin, in such a miserable voice that Beryl gave her a little shake.

Beryl saw in the visit all kinds of adventure. First, Robin must keep her eyes open and determine whether Miss Alicia Granger still mourned for young Christopher or whether she was faithless to his memory. Then there'd be the young people, probably from New York, with all kinds of new clothes and new slang and new stories of that happy whirl in which Beryl fancied all young people of wealth lived. And then there was the son, Tom. And Robin could wear the white and silver georgette dress.

"I wish it were you going instead of me," Robin mourned, not at all encouraged by Beryl's enthusiasm. "You're so tall and pretty, Beryl, and can always think of things to say."

There shone, however, one bright ray in all the gloom - the Granger home, Harkness had said, was only a mile from the Granger Mills. Adam Kraus and Dale had spoken of the Granger Mills as though they were almost perfect. She wanted to see them, at least, on the outside.

With a heart so heavy that she scarcely noticed the sheen of soft green with which the early spring had dressed the hills, Robin arrived at Wyckham, the Granger home, at tea time. She was only conscious of a wide, low door, level with the bricked terrace, flanked by stone seats; that this door opened and revealed a circle of merry-voiced young people gathered around a great fireplace. As the impressive under-butler took her bags from Williams one of the group rose quickly and came toward her. She was very tall and slender with an oval-shaped face and a prominent nose like Mrs. Granger's. Robin knew she was Miss Alicia. She answered something unintelligible to Miss Alicia's informal greeting and let herself be drawn into the circle.

There were four girls, ranging in age anywhere from sixteen to twenty - three very pretty, obviously conscious of their modish garments and wanting everyone else to be conscious of them, too; another, Rosalyn Crane, tall and tanned and strong in limb and shoulder, with frank dark eyes and red lips which smiled and displayed regular, gleaming-white teeth. Robin liked her best, and Rosalyn Crane felt this and promptly tucked Robin under her wing.

For the next several hours life moved forward for Robin at such a dizzying pace that she felt as though she were sitting apart from her body and watching her flesh-and-bones do things they had never dreamed of doing before; the noisy tea-circle, the room she shared with the nice girl, the casual welcome from Mrs. Granger, the georgette and silver dress and the silver slippers that matched, the beautiful drawing room so alive with color and jollity, the long table gleaming with crystal and silver, the voices, voices, (everyone's but hers) the bare shoulders and the bright eyes and the red, red cheeks, the

Japanese servants, velvet-footed, the big, hot-house straw-
berries, music and dancing, (everyone dancing but her) and
then, at last, bed.

Out of the whirl stood two pleasant moments: one when Mr.
Granger had spoken to her, the other - Tom.

Mr. Granger had a kind face, all criss-crossed with fine lines
that curved up when he smiled. He patted her on the shoulder
and said: "A Forsyth girl, eh?" and made Robin feel that he
liked her. And she was not afraid of him and answered easily
and not in the tongue-tied way she spoke to Miss Alicia and
her friends.

And Tom Granger looked like his father. He had a jolly way of
talking, too, and talked mostly to Rosalyn Crane. He had sat
between her and Robin at dinner and had made Robin feel
quite comfortable by acting as though they were old
acquaintances and did not need to keep up a fire of banter like
the others.

The next morning Robin came downstairs to find the house
deserted except for the noiseless butlers who stared at her as
though she were some strange freak. Apparently no one stirred
before noon, for Tom, coming in from the garage, greeted her
with a pleasant: "Say, you're an early bird, aren't you?" and
then directed one of the butlers to bring her some breakfast in
the sun-room.

"*You've* got some sense. Al's crowd will miss half of this
glorious day!" he commented, leading Robin into a glass-
enclosed room, in the centre of which splashed a jolly
fountain.

Tom sat with her while she ate the breakfast the Jap brought
on a lacquered tray. He kept up a fire of breezy talk just as
though she were the nice Rosalyn Crane. It was mostly about
the baseball nine at Hotchkiss, of which he was manager, and
the new golf holes and an inter-school swimming match and

such things, concerning which poor Robin knew nothing, but he was so boyish and jolly that Robin did not feel in the least shy or awkward.

"Say, don't you want to go with me while I try out my new car? The road toward Cornwall is good and I've bet that I can get her up to sixty. Great morning, too. Are you game?"

Robin felt game for anything that would take her away from Miss Alicia's friends - except Rosalyn. Tom took her back to the garage and tucked her into half of the low seat and climbed in beside her.

For the next two hours they tore back and forth over the Cornwall road at a pace that caught Robin's breath in her throat. Occasionally Tom talked, but most of the time he bent over the wheel, his eyes on the road ahead with a frenzied challenge in them, as though the innocent stretch of macadam was prey for his vengeance.

Just outside of the town he slowed the car down to a snail's pace.

"Some baby, isn't she?" he asked and at Robin's perplexed eyes he went off into rollicking laughter. "Why she *eats* the road! Dad said I couldn't get it out of her. I'll tell the world. Whew!"

Robin sat forward, suddenly alert.

"Are those the Mills?"

"Yep."

They were not so very unlike the Forsyth Mills - brick walls, dust, dirt, smoke, towering chimneys, and noise, noise. But beyond them and the river were rows of neat little white cottages, each with a yard, already green.

"Best mills in New England. But Dad's prouder of his model

village - as Mother calls those cottages over there - than of his profit sheet. And look at the school - Dad wanted a school good enough for his own son and daughter, but Mother wouldn't let us go. I wish she had - I'll bet there's enough good batting material right in this town to whip every nine in this part of the country. There's Dad's library, too -"

But Robin did not heed the direction of his nod. She had suddenly seen something that made her heart leap into her throat; Adam Kraus walking into the office building carrying the square box with the leather handles, which she knew contained Dale's model. He was taking it to Mr. Granger.

A panic gripped Robin. She must do something to save that model for the Forsyth Mills - she did not know just what, but *something* -

"Stop, oh, stop. Couldn't I see your - father? I'd *like* to."

Tom looked puzzled, but good-naturedly turned the car. Robin climbed out with amazing speed.

"Take me to his office, oh, *please* take me," she begged, with such earnestness that Tom wondered if she'd gone "clean dotty."

Inside the office building there was no sign of Adam Kraus, for the reason, though Robin did not know it, that it was his second visit; he was there by appointment, and he had used a stairway that led directly to Mr. Granger's office, while Tom took Robin through the main office where a neatly dressed girl blocked their way.

Mr. Granger was busy but the young lady could wait, this efficient young person informed them, quite indifferent to the fact that she addressed Thomas Granger and Gordon Forsyth. And Robin walked into an enclosure, half consulting room, half waiting room, and sat down with fast beating heart, upon a leather and mahogany chair.

"I'll wait out here 'til you see Dad," Tom told her, to her relief, and she heard him telling one of the clerks how his "baby" could make sixty as easy -

Suddenly Robin took in other voices, one deep, one soft and drawling. A door at the end of the room stood half-open. She leaned toward it, alertly listening.

"And you say this invention is your own, Kraus? Have you your patents?"

"My applications have all gone in and I have some of the patents. Yes, sir, it's my own."

"Doran reported very favorably. With one or two changes - suppose we find Doran, now." There came the sound of a chair scraping backward. "Oh, the model will be quite safe here. I want Doran to point out one or two things on our new loom. It will only take a moment. Then we'll bring him back here."

Oh, would they come out through the waiting-room - thought Robin, shrinking back. And what had Adam Kraus said?

But Mr. Granger had opened another door - Robin heard it close. She stepped noiselessly toward that half-open door at the end of the room. Her head was clear, her heart atingle.

He, Adam Kraus, had *dared* to say the invention was his! The wicked man, the traitor - to betray Dale's trust, his friendship!

The office was quite empty. And on the big desk, amid a litter of papers and letters and books and ledgers, stood the little model in its clumsy box.

Robin caught it up and held it close to her, defiantly. She snatched a pencil and scrawled a few lines on the back of an envelope, then she tiptoed out into the consulting office and on through the main office. Tom was waiting at the end of the room. It seemed to Robin as though hundreds of eyes accused her; in reality only a few lifted from the work of the day to stare at the young girl Tom Granger had brought to see his father. And if anyone wondered why she carried the queer box, no one of them was likely to presume to question any friend of the Grangers.

"Did y'see Dad?" But Tom, to Robin's relief, took that for granted and turned back to his acquaintance among the clerks.

"I'll take you out with me and *prove* it to you!"

Robin wanted to beg Tom to run but she did not dare. He asked to carry the box and she let him, for fear, if she refused, he might suspect something. Queer shivers raced up and down her spine and a dreadful sinking feeling attacked her heart and dragged at her throat so that she could scarcely speak.

He helped her into the car and climbed in himself. He leisurely experimented with the gears, until Robin almost screamed in her anxiety. Then just as he started the motor, a shout hailed them from the office door, and both turned to see Adam Kraus tearing down the steps bareheaded, wildly waving his arms, followed by a half-dozen clerks and Mr. Granger, himself.

"Go! *Go!*" implored Robin, catching his arm, and so frightened rang her voice that Tom instinctively obeyed and stepped on the accelerator with such force that the car shot forward. "Oh, *faster! Faster!*" she sobbed. "*He's coming.*" A backward glance had told her that Adam Kraus intended to give chase; still bareheaded, he had jumped into a Ford standing in the road.

"Well, I don't know what we're running away from, but my baby can give anything on wheels a good go-by!" laughed Tom, his eyes keen. He leaned over the wheel, his face fixed on the road with its "eat-her-up" tensity.

They turned into the Cornwall road. At a rise Robin saw the

other car with its bareheaded driver tearing after them.

"Oh, he's coming," she moaned, sinking down into the seat.

"Say, Miss Forsyth - I'm keen - on - running - away - but what - the - deuce - from? Who's that - fellow - following - us - why are you - afraid?" He flung the words jerkily, sideways, at Robin.

"I'll tell you - afterwards," Robin gasped back. The wind whistled past her, she lost her hat. She crouched in her seat, her hands clinging tightly to the box, her head turned as though expecting their pursuer to overtake them any moment.

Suddenly Tom frowned. At the same time the engine gave a grating "b-r-r-r."

"Oh, what is it?"

"Oil's getting low - Bad -" she caught in answer. "Pulling some - I'll - fool him, though -" He slowed down.

"Don't -" implored Robin.

"We'll turn down this road. *He'll* go straight on. Clever, eh? Say, I wouldn't have guessed you had all this spunk in you!" he took the time to say, casting her an admiring glance.

He made the turn and the "baby" ploughed through the soft rough road at a perilous clip. The road wound through thickly wooded hills, up and down, apparently leading to nowhere.

Suddenly it twisted up a long hill. Tom's car climbed easily, slackening its speed for a few moments at the top. Turning, Robin could make out the course over which they had come and, to her horror, the little car plunging over it.

"Look - *look!*" she cried.

"Well, I'll be - blowed!" Tom Granger stared as though he could not believe his eyes. "He saw the marks of my new tires, I guess. He's a sharp one. Cheer up - we're not caught yet." He increased the speed; they tore down the slope in breakneck haste.

But, in the hollow, the car slopped out of the muddy ruts, gave a sickening lurch sidewise and dropped with a jolt into mud to the axles.

His face white with excitement Tom Granger tore at the gears, tried to go back, to go forward, but in vain. And, presently, they both heard the distant throb of a motor.

Robin jumped down from the car, hugging her box. "I'll run. Good-bye, Tom, thank you *so* much!" She was far too excited to realize the familiar way in which she had addressed him. She had cleared the ditch and stood on the fringe of the deep woods.

"I'll tell you sometime - about it!" she flung to him. "I'm - not - stealing! That man - will know -" and she disappeared among the leafing undergrowth.

"Well, I'll - be - Oh, I *say*, Miss Forsyth, don't -" But the boy's attention, quite naturally, turned to meet the enemy, who at that moment appeared over the crest of the hill.

CHAPTER XXII

THE GREEN BEADS

Beryl waved Robin off to the Granger's with a forced cheerfulness. Left alone, she sat in the room she shared with Robin and stared unhappily at the disarray left from the frenzied packing and unpacking.

Nothing exciting like going off to a house-party of young people with two bags full of lovely clothes would ever, *ever* happen to her!

In fact *nothing* exciting would ever happen. She'd just go on and on wanting things all her life.

She did not envy Robin, for Robin was such a dear no one could ever envy her, but she wished she could have just *some* of the chances Robin had - and did not appreciate. She straightened. Oh, with just one of Robin's dresses, couldn't she sail into that drawing room at Wyckham and hold her own with the proudest of them? Mrs. Granger and the haughty Alicia had no terrors for *her*, and if they tried to snub her, she'd put her violin under her chin and then -

The peal of the doorbell reverberated through the quiet house. Beryl heard Harkness' slow step, as he went to the door; then it climbed the stairs and stopped outside of Robin's room.

"Miss Beryl - a telegram."

"For me?" Beryl drew back. She had never received a telegram in her life and the yellow envelope frightened her.

"The boy said as to sign here."

Beryl wrote her name mechanically in letters that zigzagged crazily. Harkness lingered while she tore open the envelope, concern struggling with curiosity on his face.

"It's from Robin's guardian. He - he wants - oh, Harkness, am I reading *right*? He says I must come to New York at *once* - tonight, if I can. He'll meet me - it's *extremely* important. Why, Harkness, what in the world has happened? It doesn't sound awful, does it? Did you ever know of anything so mysterious in your life?"

Harkness never had. He read the telegram with brows drawn together.

"Mebbe they left out something," he suggested, turning the sheet and scrutinizing its back.

"Well, I'll *have* to go." Beryl's voice betrayed her deep excitement. "I *can* catch the evening train. Oh, Harkness, how often I've watched that go out and wished I was on it! And now I'm going to be. I'm going to New York! Harkness, be a *dear* and hurry some dinner, will you? I'll pack. And oh, will you take a note to mother for me? I'll not have time to stop. Or wait - I won't tell her I'm going until I know what it's for - she'd worry. Isn't that best?"

"Yes, that's best. I'll get you some nice dinner, don't you fret. And Joe'll take you down to the station in the truck, he will, for like as not he'll be meetin' the train anyways for his wife's niece who lives Boston way. She's a-goin' to help Joe's wife -"

"Oh, that'll be *nice*. But please hurry, Harkness. That boy's waiting for his book. And I can't think."

Two hours later Beryl sat upright on the plush seat of the evening train, her old suitcase at her feet packed with every garment she possessed.

"This is more fun than all your old house-parties," she apostrophized the black square of window, which dimly reflected her glowing face. Then she lost herself in a delicious "I wonder" as to why she had been summoned so mysteriously to New York.

Cornelius Allendyce and Miss Effie met her at the end of her wonderful journey, no part of which had wearied her in the least, and their smiling faces put at rest the tiny misgiving that had persisted that she might be walking into some sort of a scheme to separate her from Robin.

"I am glad you got my telegram in time to catch tonight's train. I've made an important appointment for you tomorrow morning with a friend of mine." But not another word concerning the mystery would the lawyer say. Both he and his sister went about with a queer smile, and treated Beryl as fond (and rich) parents might a good child on Christmas Eve.

The next morning Miss Effie started the two of them off for the "appointment" with a fluttery excitement bordering on hysteria.

"You'll think, my dear, you've rubbed Aladdin's lamp," she whispered to Beryl, patting down the neat white collar of Beryl's coat.

Beryl thought of her words when she followed Mr. Allendyce through a long dim room, crowded with treasures of fabric and ceramic, rich in coloring, fragrant of oriental perfumes.

"He's a collector," Cornelius Allendyce explained, nodding sideways and hurrying on to a room in the back, as though their errand had nothing to do with the curious things about them.

"Ah, there, Eugene, we're here! Miss Lynch, this is Eugene Dominez, known to two continents as that rare specimen, an honest collector; to me, the only man I can't beat at chess!"

A very small man rose from a great carved chair. He had a thin, leathery face with an exaggerated nose, stretched out as though from sniffing for curios in dusty dim corners. When he smiled his eyes shut and his mouth twisted until he looked like a jolly little gnome.

"Ah-ha! You admit you cannot beat me!" He spoke with a soft accent. "And this is the little lady who owns the green beads." And he peered closely at Beryl.

The green beads! She had not thought of them once.

"Sit down. Sit down. I will ask you to tell me a story. Then I will tell *you* a story. First, my dear young lady, tell me where you found the beads?" As he spoke, he drew open a drawer, and took from it the envelope Robin had given to her guardian.

Beryl answered briefly, for the simple reason that she found difficulty managing her tongue.

"An - an old priest - back in Ireland - gave them - to us. He'd found them in an antique shop in London."

"Ah, so! Just so! So! So!" crowed the gnome-like man, jumping up and down in his great chair. "Now I will tell *you* a story."

"Once upon a time, as you say, a beautiful Queen of the fifteenth century, while travelling through a forest, came upon a roving band of gypsies. So great was her beauty that the gypsy chief gave to her a necklace of precious jade, upon each bead of which had been tooled a crown, so infinitesimal as to be seen only through a strong lens. The chief told the fair Queen that the necklace brought good fortune to whosoever possessed it. But so proud was the young Queen of the precious beads and the good fortune that was to be hers that she boasted of them to her Court and aroused the envy of many until a knave among her courtiers stole them from her. For generations these beads, the workmanship of a Magyar artisan, have passed from owner to owner, always mysteriously, for, because of the good fortune they had power to bestow, no one parted with them except from the most dire necessity, and only lost them through theft. Ah," he held up one of the glowing green globes, "the stories they could tell of greed and dishonor and cunning! The lies that have been told for them! And an old priest found them at last! It is many years since there has been any trace." He stared at Beryl as though to see through her into the past. Then he roused quickly and shook his shoulders. "They have hung about the necks of crowned people, good people - and wicked people. Perhaps they have brought good fortune - as the Magyar chieftain said they would. Who knows? You, my dear - you are a girl with a sensible head on a pair of straight shoulders - tell me, do you care more for the superstition of this necklace - than for the money I will pay you for it - say, fifteen thousand dollars?"

Beryl stood up so suddenly that her chair tumbled backward, making a crashing noise in the subdued stillness of the little room.

"Are you joking?" she asked in a queer, choky voice.

"No, he is not joking. And I told you he is known the world over as an honest collector," broke in Cornelius Allendyce.

"Fifteen - thousand - dollars! Why, that's an *awfully* big amount, isn't it?" Beryl appealed helplessly to the lawyer. "Why - of *course* I'll sell it - if you're sure it's what you think it is. I - I don't want -"

The little collector handed her one of the beads and a strong magnifying glass. "Look!" he commanded. Beryl obeyed. There, quite plainly, she made out a tiny crown.

She laughed hysterically. "I see it! I thought that was a scratch. I never noticed it was on every one. Oh, how queer! A queen wore these!" She rolled the bead slowly in the palm of her hand. Then she handed it back. "But I'd much rather have the money than the beads even if a dozen queens wore them." Her sound practicalness rang harshly in the exotic atmosphere of the room.

"I explained to Mr. Dominez your situation - and your ambition," Cornelius Allendyce put in almost apologetically.

"Mr. Allendyce will represent you in this deal, Miss Lynch, if you care to think the sale over. However, I am giving you a final offer. You are young and -"

Beryl reached out both hands with childish impulsiveness. "Oh, I want the money *now!* I want to spend it. I want - oh, you don't *know* all I want -" She stopped abruptly, confused by the smiles on both men's faces.

"Mr. Dominez will give you a partial payment in cash and the rest I will deposit in the bank to your credit," explained Cornelius Allendyce. "You need not feel ashamed of your excitement, my dear; fortune like this does not come often to anyone. It's hard, indeed, not to believe that the little beads *have* magic."

"I'm dreaming. I'm just *plain dreaming* and I'll wake up in a minute and find I'm Beryl Lynch, poor as ever!" Beryl whispered to herself as she followed Robin's guardian out into the sunshine of the street. She felt of her bulging pocketbook, into which she had put the roll of bills the little collector had smilingly given her, and which Robin's guardian had counted over, quite seriously. It felt real but it just *couldn't* be true -

"Now where, my dear? You ought to make this day one you'll never forget."

"Don't I have to go right back to Wassumsic? Oh, then - then

- can I go to see Jacques Henri and tell him? I know the way - I can take the Ninth Avenue Elevated - or - Would it be *very* foolish if I took a taxi?" Beryl colored furiously.

"Not at all, Miss Beryl, not at all. Take the taxi and keep it there to return to my house; then you and Miss Effie put your heads together and decide just what you want to do first with your money."

Beryl rejoiced that it was a nice shiny taxi, quite like a real lady's car. She sniffed delightedly the leathery smell, sat bolt upright with her chin in the air.

"Go straight down Fifth Avenue," she instructed the driver.

Spring, with its eternal sorcery, caressed the great city. Its spell threw a sheen over the drab things Beryl remembered so well, the brick schoolhouse, the Settlement, the dirty narrow street flanked by dull-brown tenements with their endless fire escapes mounting higher and higher, hung now with bedding of every color. The street swarmed with children returning from school, and they gathered about the automobile climbing on to the running board on either side and peering through the windows.

"It's the Lynch girl," someone cried and another answered jeeringly.

"Aw, git off! Wot she doin' in this swell autymobile?"

Beryl did not mind in the least the street urchins; even though she had lived among them, neither she nor Dale had ever been of them, thanks to her mother's watchful care. She smiled at them and fled into the dark alley way that led to the court which, all through her childhood, had been her playground.

As she climbed, a dreadful thought appalled her. What if dear old Jacques Henri had moved away - or died! But, no, at the very moment she let the fear halt her climbing step she heard the dear sound of his violin. She crept to his door and softly opened it.

The old man stood near his window, through which he could see a slit of blue sky between two walls. On the sill were the pink geraniums he nursed through winter and summer, their pinkness brightening the gloom of the bare, dim room. Jacques Henri called them his family.

"Jacques Henri!" Beryl ran to him and threw her strong arms about him.

"Hold! Let me look. My girl? Ah, do my old eyes tell me false things? No, it's my little Beryl!"

Beryl took his violin from him, kissed its strings lightly and laid it carefully upon the table. Then she pushed the startled old man back into the one comfortable chair and perched herself upon its arm.

"Listen, dear Jacques Henri, and I'll tell you the strangest story that you ever heard - about Queens and gypsies and green beads and a girl you know. Don't say *one* word until I'm through." And Beryl told in all its wonderful detail, the happenings of the morning.

"And don't you see what it means? I can begin to study at *once*! Right this minute! And, *oh*, how I'll work and practice and learn until -"

She caught up the old man's violin and its bow and drew it across the strings.

"Play!" commanded Jacques Henri, without so much as a word for the Aladdin-lamp tale she had told him.

Beryl played and as she played she wished with all her might she could summon the power that had been hers on Christmas night. She wanted to play for Jacques Henri as she had played then. But she could not.

"Stop!"

Beryl laid the violin down.

The old man scowled at her until she shifted nervously under his searching eyes.

"Your fingers - they are clever, your ear is true - but there is nothing - of *you* - in what you play! Do you know what I mean?"

He did not wait for Beryl to answer; he went on, with a shake of his great head and his eyes still fixed upon her.

"You come to me and tell me your good fortune and what you will do; how *you* can study and *you* can work and *you* can learn to make good music - and you have no word for what that money will mean to your saint of a mother - aye, the best woman God ever made! Shame to you, selfish girl, that you should put your ambition before her dreams!"

The color dyed Beryl's face. "I never thought -" she muttered, then stopped abruptly, ashamed of her own admission.

"No, you never thought! Do you ever think much beyond yourself?" Then, afraid that he had spoken too harshly, he laid his hand affectionately upon Beryl's shoulder. "But you are young, my dear, and youth is careless. Jacques Henri knows that there is good in you - my eyes are wise and I can see into your heart. It is an honest little heart - you will heed in time. Ambition is a greedy thing - watch out that you keep it in your clever head and do not let it wrap its hard sinews about your heart, crushing all that is beautiful there. Listen to me, child; think you that your music can reach into the souls of people if you do not feel that music in your own good soul? Your fingers may be clever and your body strong, but your music will be cold, cold, if the heart inside you is a little, cold, mean thing!

Many's the one, I grant you, content to feed the passing plaudits of the crowd, but not the master - he must go further, he must give of himself to all that they may carry something beautiful of his gift away in their hearts. *that* is the master. *that* is music."

Beryl, always so ready in self-defense, stood mute before the old man's charge. She had been scolded too often by this dear recluse to resent it; she had, too, faith in anything he might say.

Then: "You just ought to know Robin," she burst out, irrelevantly, eager that her old teacher should believe that, even though she might be a selfish, thoughtless girl herself, she could recognize and respect the good qualities in others.

"Forgive your old friend if he has hurt you. Go now to your blessed mother and lay your good fortune at her feet. That I might see her face!"

"And if she wants to use - *some* of the money, will you help me?" asked Beryl, in a meek voice.

"Ah, most surely. And proudly."

Beryl rode back to Miss Erne's in a contritely humble mood.

"I wish there were some sort of medicine one could take to make them better inside their hearts! I wouldn't care *how* nasty it tasted," she mourned, impatient at the long, hard climb that must be hers if she ever made of herself what her Jacques Henri wanted.

All of Miss Effie's coaxing could not keep Beryl from taking the afternoon train to Wassumsic.

"I must tell my mother about the beads - at once!" she answered, firmly.

CHAPTER XXIII

ROBIN'S RESCUE

Just as the shrill of the train whistle echoed through the little valley, Moira Lynch set her lighted lamp in the window. She did not sing tonight as she performed the customary ceremony, nor had she for many nights. Her throat seemed too tired, her arms dropped with the weight of her lamp, a dull little pain at the back of her neck gripped her with a pulling clutch.

The doctor had told her she was "tired out." She had gone to him very secretly, lest Dale or big Danny should know and worry. But even to be "just tired out" was very terrifying to Mother Moira - if her arms and head and heart failed, who would take care of big Danny and keep a little home for Dale and watch over Beryl?

With her habitual optimism she tried to laugh away her alarm, but the pulling ache persisted and her arms trembled under tasks that before had seemed as nothing. She told herself that it was all her own fault that her big Danny seemed harder to please, but when, under a particularly trying moment, she broke down and cried, she knew she was reaching the end of her endurance.

"Did the train stop?" queried big Danny.

"Sure and it did!" cried Mrs. Moira, trying to throw

Jane Abbott

excitement into her voice to please the invalid man. Big Danny took childish pleasure in listening for the incoming and New York-bound trains.

"What's keeping Dale? Prob'bly hanging 'round the Inn!"

Mrs. Moira smothered the quick retort that sprang to her lips in defense of her boy.

"He'll be here any minute," she said instead, comfortingly. "There he is now!" Her quick ear had caught a step outside.

Beryl, not Dale, opened the door and confronted them. Suppressed excitement, impatience, eagerness, an inward disgust of herself for being a "selfish thing anyway" combined to give Beryl's face such an unnatural pallor and haggard tensity of expression that big Danny whirled his chair toward her and Mrs. Lynch caught her hands over her heart.

"Beryl?" she cried, standing quite still.

Beryl walked to her and very quietly gathered her into her young arms.

"Don't look so scared, Mom, dear. Oh, *don't* cry! Why, I'm near crying myself! After I've told you all that has happened I shall just *bawl*. I'm too dreadfully happy. Sit down here, Mom, and hold my hand tight. Wait - I must take my things off first."

In a twinkling she had her stage "set" for her surprise. Strangely stirred herself, she had to gulp once or twice before she could begin her story. It was difficult to keep it coherent, too, because Mrs. Moira interrupted her so often with little unnecessary questions.

"Did you really go to New York?"

"And 'twas all night you stayed at the Allendyces themselves?"

Because of her mother's agitation, Beryl abandoned the details with which she had planned to lead up to the great surprise. She plunged abruptly to the point of the story.

"Those beads. They *weren't* just plain beads. They were a precious necklace made by some queer people, ages and ages ago. *Queens* have worn 'em and all sorts of wicked people and they've gone from hand to hand - I s'pose I ought to say neck to neck - for all these years and then, suddenly, no one could find them. And Mr. Allendyce's friend - the collector - gave me *this money* outright for them and -"

Mrs. Lynch suddenly sprang to furious life. She stood erect, her eyes flashing, her fingers working in and out, her lips trembling.

"You sold my - *you sold my beads!* Beryl Lynch, how *dared* you. My - my -"

Beryl stared at her. She could not speak for sheer amazement.

"My beads! They - were - the last - thing - I - had that held - me - to - my - dreams." Her voice died off in a heart-broken whisper that hurt Beryl to the soul.

"Mother! Mother, *please* don't. It isn't too late. I can get them back. I didn't know you cared, don't you see?"

Beryl of course did not know about the pulling ache at the back of Mother Moira's neck or she would have understood that her mother's hysteria was due partly to that. She had never seen her mother look so queer and old and pale and it frightened her.

Mrs. Lynch crossed the room until she stood behind Danny's chair. Involuntarily her hand moved to his shoulder.

"No, you wouldn't know. It isn't your fault. Of course it's just beads they were, but they belonged to the young part of me when my heart was that light and full of beautiful dreams and so strong that it hurt the inside of me. And nothing in this world was too fine for the likes of my Danny and me. And we thought 'twas just ours for the asking. And then when the clouds come -" her hand pressed big Danny's shoulder ever so lightly, "I told myself the dreams were my own and no one could *take them* away from me and if I couldn't make them come true, as true for himself and me, sure, I'd keep them for my boy and girl. And 'twas the beads were like a dear voice out of the past telling me to be strong, for Father Murphy, with the saints in Heaven now, God rest him, gave them to me himself with his blessing and saying might my dreams come true! Ah, well - sure it's a punishment, maybe, for me wanting things just for my own -"

"Mother!" broke in Beryl, sternly. "As if you could be punished for anything! Will you tell me one thing? Which would you rather have - those beads - or - or - a nice little farm in the hills with a cow and chickens and pigs and a little orchard and - and a Ford - and a girl to do the cooking so's you could stay with Pop, and Dale studying engineering in some college, if he wanted to, and me -"

"Beryl Lynch, are ye crazy?" cried big Danny, suspecting that the girl was in someway trying to mock her mother.

"*No*, I'm not crazy, though I ought to be, with old Jacques Henri scolding me and now mother -" She bit her lip childishly. "Will you please just answer me, mother?"

"A farm - with a garden - and a cow - and trees and a good stretch of the green meadow - ah, sure I'd think it a bit of Heaven."

"Mother, you can have it! You can have it!" Beryl rushed to and knelt by big Danny's chair. "That's what I was trying to tell you. That man will give you fifteen thousand dollars for those beads! Really, truly. See, he gave me all this money today. And Mr. Allendyce will put the rest in the bank. Oh, I know it's hard to believe but it's true. You can ask Mr. Allendyce."

Big Danny, with trembling hands, took the roll of bills from Beryl's purse. They were undisputable proof of her story.

"Moira girl, 'tis true!" Big Danny's voice trembled.

"'Tis Father Murphy's blessing," whispered Mrs. Lynch, a strange light in her eyes. "May I be worthy of it!" Then she roused and laughed, a tinkling laugh. "Ah - my girl shall have her music, now! Oh, it's too wonderful."

"Where's Dale?" cried Beryl, her heart jubilant that the unexpected crisis had passed. "Won't he be surprised?"

"What ever can be keeping the boy? 'Tis long past the hour."

"Now, mother, don't you begin a-worrying. Dale's old enough to look after himself."

"It's a fussing old hen I am, as true as true!" And because once more her heart was so light inside of her that it hurt, she kissed her big Danny on the top of his head.

"I wish Dale would come. I ought to go back to the Manor. Harkness is probably worrying his head off over my strange visit to New York."

But Harkness had other things to worry about.

Dale burst in upon his family just a few moments after Beryl had spoken but she did not tell her story. He gave her no opportunity.

"Gordon Forsyth's lost!"

"*Lost?*"

"Yes. Somewhere in the woods between Cornwall and South Falls. Strangest thing you ever heard. She made young Tom Granger run off with her - goodness knows where they were headed for, and when his car went into the ditch she made a dash for the woods and that's the last anyone's seen of her."

"Why, Dale, she couldn't -" cried Beryl.

"Couldn't? Easiest thing in the world. Woods are thick and miles deep through there."

"I mean she couldn't be running off with Tom Granger. Why, she never met him until yesterday -"

"Well, it wasn't exactly *with* him but she made him, *take* her off. She was running away from some one. Granger's been over here talking to Norris. They called me in. Seems Kraus had taken my model to sell to Granger, and called it his own, and Miss Gordon heard him. And she just walked in when they weren't in the room and - took it. Granger wouldn't say any more. He's too worried. What I think is that Kraus chased them - Miss Gordon and Tom Granger -"

"How *thrilling! What* an adventure," exclaimed Beryl, her eyes shining. Oh, exciting things *were* happening!

"Thrilling! Won't be thrilling if anything's happened to the kid. It's four hours now and Granger's had a bunch of men hunting ever since his son walked into the office and gave the alarm. Can you give me a bite in a hurry, Mom? The Manor car's going to take six of us over to meet young Granger and make a thorough search."

"But it's tired to death you look now, Dale. Can't -"

"I'm not tired - just bothered. Mom, I hate to think of that little thing getting into this fix just for my model. Granger was awfully decent about the thing; told Norris he was a fool not to jump at it. He said he had some sort of a note Miss Robin had left and it seemed to amuse him, but he didn't offer to show it. It isn't only because she's a Forsyth I care, but she's such a square little thing. Hurry up, please, Mom, Williams may stop any moment."

"*I* ought to go up to the Manor. They must be in an awful state."

"Wait, as soon as ever I can fix your father I'll go with you myself," cried Mrs. Lynch.

*   *   *   *   *

Toward noon of the next day, in answer to an urgent telegram, Cornelius Allendyce arrived at the Manor, having come down from New York by motor. Just as he was gulping down the coffee Harkness had brought to him, Mr. Granger, Senior, was ushered in.

The men knew one another well. They shook hands, then Cornelius Allendyce motioned him to a chair opposite him at the table.

The lawyer only needed to look at the other man's face to know that he brought no good news.

"Tom telephoned from Cornwall at six o'clock. Not a sign. Not so much as a red hair! Strangest thing I ever heard of. They're going to search the ravines today - easy enough for her to stumble into them if she was frightened or hurrying. Then there's the kidnapping possibility!"

"Improbable!" protested the lawyer.

"Well, *nothing's* improbable. You'd have said it wasn't to be thought of that a youngster like that would run off with that model. I want to give you the details of this whole matter - they'd be extremely interesting if one were not so concerned." He told of his two interviews with Adam Kraus and of Dale's invention. "A master contrivance. I can't understand your man, here, letting it get away from him. Why, it's worth a lot to me, but in these Mills - well, you may not know what I think of your mills," he laughed. "I'll tell you another time. The girl saw this Kraus go into my office, and persuaded my boy, who'd been taking her for a ride, to stop. She was waiting in my outer office and heard Kraus claim the invention as his own - scoundrel that he was - and when I took Kraus to see my head foreman, didn't she walk in, help herself to the model and leave me this." He drew an envelope from his pocket and handed it to Cornelius Allendyce. "Read it."

"This model is Dale Lynch's. I am taking it to him. When I see my guardian, I shall make him buy it for the Forsyth Mills.

GORDON FORSYTH."

Cornelius Allendyce looked up from the bit of paper. He had suddenly recalled the frightened little girl he had first brought to Gray Manor.

"Who'd believe that the child had the nerve?"

"That's what I said. Well, she ran off with it, Kraus gave chase, Tom headed toward Cornwall, then switched off on an unimproved road and came to grief. Just as Kraus was about to overtake them the child ran off into the wood. Tom didn't have the vaguest idea what it was all about, but he tried to head off Kraus and when Kraus started for the wood he did a little wrestling trick that surprised the fellow, got him down, tied him in the Ford and went himself in search of Miss Gordon. When he came back after an hour's search he found Kraus and the Ford gone and he walked back to South Falls. That's all."

"That model may be worth a lot, but it is not worth another tragedy to this house," groaned Cornelius Allendyce.

"No. It is worth a good deal - but not - that much."

A few moments' deep silence prevailed. Wrinkles of worry twisted the lawyer's face. What a mess it all was, anyway - he had urged Robin to go to the Granger's in hopes that she'd bring the two families into close intimacy again and instead of that she had gotten herself into this fix. If they found her safe and sound she ought to be spanked and taught to keep her hands off the Mill affairs until she was older. But down in his heart he knew this was only a vexatious expression of his concern - you couldn't punish Robin for anything.

"As her guardian I appreciate your alarm. I share it with you, not alone because Miss Forsyth was a guest at my house but because I took a great fancy to the child. It struck me, as I looked at her, that her coming to Wassumsic - to the Manor, might change things, here, quite a bit."

"It has - it will," mumbled Mr. Allendyce. For a moment, just to relieve his feelings, he wondered if he might not confide in this very human man the ordeal he must face with Madame Forsyth when his reckoning came.

"My wife is prostrated with it all. She does not know the particulars but she is deeply concerned. I do not like to add to your worry but do you think there is any possibility that the child returned to the road, and that Kraus, freed from Tom's rope, captured her and went off with her?"

"Why, every possibility in the world!" shouted Robin's guardian. "Why did you hug that idea to yourself? We'll telephone the New York police. He's sure to make straight for the city."

Both men welcomed action. They rushed to the library and put in a long distance call and then, while waiting, paced the room's length back and forth. Harkness, shaking and white and miserable, glued his ear to the crack in the door, hopeful for one crumb of comforting news.

Below stairs Mrs. Budge, flatly refusing to believe that "Miss Robin" could be lost just when she had learned to love her, beat up a cake for her homecoming, unmindful of the tears that splashed into the batter.

In the little sitting-room they had shared, Beryl, who did not even have the heart to play with Susy, sat with her nose against the window watching the ribbon of road over which anyone would come if they came. That was why she was the first of the Manor household to spy the dilapidated Ford approaching, snorting up the incline. Something about it made her think of the general dilapidation of the Forgotten Village. It might be some word! She rushed down the stairs, two steps at a time, past the startled Harkness, through the big front door. The strange-looking car had turned into the Manor gate. A man with long white whiskers was driving it. And yes, a bareheaded girl, who looked like Robin, sat on the back seat. It *was* Robin. Beryl waved her hand wildly and Robin answered. But who rode with her? Beryl's flying feet came to a quick halt.

"As sure as I'm *alive* it's the Queen of Altruria!"

Turning, Beryl rushed back to the Manor.

"Harkness! *Harkness!*" she cried, bursting in through the door. "Robin's coming! She's *here!* And she's brought the Queen of Altruria with her! Oh, *what'll* we do?" For surely some ceremony befitting royalty should be prepared.

"The Queen of *what* -" cried Mr. Granger and Cornelius Allendyce rushing from the library. "Oh, the girl's *crazy* -" asserted the lawyer. Nevertheless he ran to the door, followed by Mr. Granger and Harkness and Beryl and Hannah Budge and Chloe, who had heard Beryl's glad cry in the kitchen.

At close range the dilapidated Ford looked even more dilapidated; Robin, letting her royal companion talk terms of payment with the bewhiskered scion of the Forgotten Village, clambered out the moment the car stopped and fell into

Beryl's arms. From their shelter, after the briefest instant, she lifted her face to greet her guardian and found him staring at the Queen in a sort of stupid unbelief.

"I brought -" Robin started an introduction, but did not finish. For, recovering, with an obvious effort, his natural manner of politeness, her guardian was hurrying down the steps to the little car.

"Madame Forsyth, I did not expect -"

CHAPTER XXIV

MADAME FORSYTH COMES HOME

"No. I judge from all your faces no one expected me!" exclaimed Madame Forsyth coldly, extending to Cornelius Allendyce the tips of her fingers. "Harkness, you look as though you were seeing a ghost!"

Her rebuking words had the effect of galvanizing poor Harkness' limbs to action - but not his tongue. Though he hobbled down the steps and took the bag from the lawyer's hand, not a word could he speak from sheer stupefaction.

And Hannah Budge so forgot her long years of loyalty to the House of Forsyth as to cry out - "Oh, Miss Robin!" before so much as one word of greeting for Madame Forsyth.

"You could 'a clean knocked me over," she explained to Harkness afterward, "Our Madame going away as fine as you please with that baggage of a Florrie who was as full of tricks as a cat after a mouse, and coming back in that old car that had moss on it, I do believe, and with Miss Robin, too, who they all thought was lost though *I* knew better. Something *told* me to beat up that cake yesterday!"

"And Miss Robin didn't know Madame was Madame," explained Harkness, his face perplexed. "She and Miss Beryl here've been thinking she was some mysterious lydy or other - Williams says they got it in their little heads she was a

Queen hiding -"

"Madame hiding *where?*" snorted Budge.

"Well, *I* can't make nothing out of it. My head goes 'round in a circle like. Only Williams says that lydy must be the lydy the young lydies visited, mysterious like, just afore Christmas and the lydy's our Madame all right and that's what I say my head goes 'round in a circle!"

"Your tongue, too, Timothy Harkness. Well, there's lots going to happen now, or my name ain't Hannah Budge. First thing, I s'pose, she'll clear that Castle young 'un out of the house and then your Miss Beryl. And mebbe send Miss Robin off to school somewheres to get these common notions out o' her little head. You say they're all talking upstairs now?"

"Only Madame and the lawyer man. Mr. Granger's gone down to the Mills to send word to his home that Miss Robin's found."

"Saints be praised!" murmured Mrs. Budge, devoutly.

Up in her little sitting-room Robin and Beryl sat arm in arm, and Robin told Beryl the whole story of her adventure. On the window seat beside them lay the square box containing Dale's model.

"I just ran, Beryl, as fast as I could and *anywhere*. I was so frightened I didn't stop to look. I fell down twice and the second time I was so tired I could scarcely get up. But I had to. And then I thought I'd found a path, and I followed it, but it stopped at a ravine that was, *oh*, so deep. Well, I knew I was lost. I called and called and no one answered. And I heard all sorts of queer noises as though there might be wild beasts. One came very close, I'm sure, though I couldn't see it. And I was dreadfully hungry. I sat down on a log and cried, too - my feet ached so and my arms ached so from carrying this box. I decided to bury it and leave a note telling about it, for, honestly, Beryl, I didn't think then I'd live an hour longer, but I didn't have a pencil and when I started to dig with my hands the ground was so gooy that I couldn't bear to. Oh, I'll never forget it." She shuddered and Beryl held her hands tighter. "And it began to get dark. I tried to be brave and say nothing could hurt me, but I couldn't help but hear the funny noises and I was so *awfully* alone. I started to walk again, just somewhere, because when I walked I couldn't hear all the sounds and every now and then I'd call out. And just as it was almost pitch dark in the wood something big came rushing toward me and sprang at me and, Beryl, I fainted dead away! Well, the next thing I knew something was licking my face. And someone was saying something queer, and Beryl, it was Caesar and that Brina from our House of Rushing Water! Caesar had heard me call and found me, and then he had barked and howled until Brina came with a lantern."

Beryl jumped up and down in excitement.

"What happened then?" she cried.

"Brina carried me - and that box - to the house in the wood. It seemed I'd gotten most to it and didn't know it. And the Queen was awfully frightened. But she wouldn't let me say a word; she made Brina put me in her bed and she covered me with blankets and she fed me herself, something hot and oh, so good. And she kept petting me and cuddling me for I guess I shook like a leaf. You see, I couldn't *believe* I was safe and sound; I kept seeing that dog jump at me! And finally she sang to me, the nicest old-fashioned song and I went to sleep, and I never opened my eyes until this morning, and there she stood by my bed with a tray of nice breakfast. She wouldn't let me tell her how I got lost until I'd eaten every crumb. And then I felt so cosy and warm and safe that I told her everything - *everything*, all about Mother Lynch and how my plans for the House of Laughter had failed at first, and then the Rileys and what I thought of the Mills, and how horrid Mr. Norris was and about Susy and poor Granny and Dale's model, and then what I'd done at Grangers'. I just got started and I couldn't stop. And Beryl, I told her *again* how my aunt was an unhappy old woman who worried over her own troubles so much that she didn't have time for other people's. Wasn't that dreadful?" And Robin caught up a pillow and buried her face in it.

Beryl looked troubled.

"Yes, that *was* dreadful. What ever did she say?"

"She didn't say anything. She picked up my tray and went out, and I felt the way I had that other time, all fussed, because I'd bothered a Queen with my silly affairs. And I could have sworn then she was a Queen, Beryl, she had such a dignified way of being sweet and she smelled so nice and perfumy - a different perfume. And that Brina had put the gorgeousest nightgown on me, too."

"When did you first know the Queen was your aunt?" Beryl broke in.

"Beryl Lynch, on my honor, not until my guardian called her Madame Forsyth! After she took my tray out she came back, and she did look sort of funny, now I remember, the way one does when one decides suddenly to do something you hadn't dreamed of doing, and she told me Brina had gone into the village to hunt up some sort of a vehicle to get me back to the Manor. And I didn't think until the last moment that she meant to come, too. And all the way over I was nearly bursting thinking how surprised you'd be and what fun it would be to have the Queen visit us. Oh, dear!" And Robin drew a long breath, half sigh.

"Well, something'll happen *now*," groaned Beryl, in much the same tone Budge had used. "When she finds out about Susy and me!"

And below in the library the same thought held Robin's guardian - something must happen, now.

He had gone there to wait while Madame Forsyth freshened herself after her long ride. And while he waited, in considerable apprehension, he planned the course he would follow; if Madame refused to accept little Red-Robin as her heir, because she was a girl and *different*, why, he'd take her back with him to his own home. She could live with him and his sister until Jimmie came back and he'd even adopt her if Jimmie would let him. And he'd take Beryl, too, if Robin wished - and he'd see Susy was put with some nice family.

But where in the world had Robin found her aunt - or her aunt found Robin. Everyone acted as though they were knocked stupid by the mystery - no one had offered a word of explanation. He rubbed his forehead as though it might have circles, too.

"Which shall we hear first?" a voice asked behind him, "How *you* happened to bring little Robin here - or how *I* did?"

The words startled him more because of their tone than their unexpectedness. And turning, he saw (to his immense relief) that Madame Forsyth was smiling - and in her eyes was a softened look, though they were shadowed with fatigue.

"I am immensely curious, I must admit, as to where you found Robin, but I feel that I owe you the first explanation."

He told then, of his first visit to Patchin Place and of his finding little Robin in her curious surroundings.

"I really cannot say just what put the notion in my head of taking her to the Manor - I think it was something appealing about the child."

"You are more honest to admit that than I expected, Cornelius Allendyce. Your silence in regard to her being a girl might seem inexcusable to me only that I am glad, now, that you kept silence. For I would have most certainly, then, sent her back. And - I am glad that never happened. You see *I* can be honest, too."

"Before I can explain my finding the child in this last plight of hers I must tell you a little of my 'wanderings' since I left the Manor. They were not far. I went to New York and reserved passage on a steamer sailing for the Mediterranean the next week. That evening I saw the 'for sale' notice of a house in the Connecticut woods, which advertised absolute seclusion. I telephoned to my banker, who has been in my confidence, and he made a hurried trip to Brown's Mill and bought the house, just as it stood. The next day I discharged Florrie, cancelled my sailing reservations, picked up a strong German woman for a cook, bought a dog and rode out to my new home. It offered all that I had hoped it would. There I planned to find a change that would be a rest, to forget the world about me and live in my past, which was all I had. And for several weeks I did - until two girls broke in upon my precious privacy."

She told of Robin and Beryl's first visit and then of their second, and of the gifts they brought from the Manor.

"I confess it was a shock to me to discover that this child was – Gordon Forsyth. Yet it was the shock I needed to rouse me from my depression. For, like you, I fell quickly under the girl's charm. From that day on I found I could not hold my thoughts to my past - in spite of me they persisted in dwelling upon the present - and the future. You see I am frank with you."

Cornelius Allendyce nodded. He dared not speak for he did not want to betray the relief he felt.

"I do not think I would have returned to the Manor for several weeks yet, for my health has singularly benefited by my - unusual change, except that this escapade of Robin's made me feel that I was needed here. Something she said made up my mind for me, rather quickly. Cornelius Allendyce - that child has a great gift. It is the gift of giving. An unusual talent in the Forsyth family, you are thinking! But like all talents it ought to be trained and directed and strengthened and my work is - to do it. I had thought my life lived - but it is not, and I am happy to have found it so. I am too old, perhaps, to learn the new ways but I am not too old to safeguard them."

"You are a wonderful old woman," the lawyer answered, quite involuntarily and with such instant alarm at his audacity that Madame Forsyth smiled.

"Oh, no. I am not wonderful at all. I am revealing my heart to you, now, in a way I do not often open it, but I shall, to my last day, probably, be a proud, overbearing old woman with a sharp tongue. You, however, will know what is underneath."

There was a moment's silence, then Madame Forsyth told him of Caesar's finding Robin in the woods and giving the alarm.

"The child was utterly exhausted. I cannot bear to think of what might have happened if we - had not been living there. Thank God we found her. May I summon the girls? I am curious to see more of this rather unusual young person my niece has attached to my household."

Then the lawyer remembered Beryl's great good fortune and that nothing had been said concerning that. How happy Robin would be!

In answer to Madame's summons Robin and Beryl came to the library, nervously sedate in manner and with fingers intertwined in a close grip.

Madame beckoned to them with her jeweled white hand.

"Come to me, Robin. Are you sorry to find that your mysterious friend by the Rushing Waters - is your aunt?"

Robin advanced slowly, her eyes on her aunt's face.

"No, oh, no! Only - maybe *you're* sorry about - *me* - being a girl and such a small one - and lame, too -"

"Oh, my *dear*!" And Madame Forsyth held out her arms impulsively and Robin, her face aglow, snuggled into them.

Every moment of that day something exciting and significant seemed to happen. Ever so many people called, and it was fun to see their surprise at finding Madame home. Aunt Mathilde, (Robin could not make the name sound natural) upon introduction, had acted as though she almost liked Susy, and Susy had looked very cunning in the new dress the nurse had made for her. And she hadn't said Susy would have to go! Then Robin flew off, the very first moment, with Beryl to find Mrs. Lynch and *hug* her over the wonderful fortune and talk about the farm which must be very near Wassumsic. Then Beryl played for Aunt Mathilde and Aunt Mathilde had looked as though she "felt funny inside!"

And then Dale had come with Tom Granger, both of them looking haggard from anxiety and lack of sleep. They came in while Beryl was playing. Robin was glad of that for it gave her a moment to think what she must say to Tom Granger in explanation.

She did not need to say anything, however. Tom knew the whole story, from his father and from Dale. He and Dale had become fast friends.

He caught Robin's hand and pumped her small arm until it ached.

"I had to see you to believe you'd turned up," he laughed. "You certainly gave us a scare we won't forget in a hurry! But you're a good little sport and I'm coming around, if I may, to take you for a ride - before I have to go back to school."

"Well, I never want to go *fast* again in my life," cried Robin, coloring under the meaning glance Beryl shot at her.

Dale greeted her more shyly, and because Madame Forsyth and Cornelius Allendyce were talking to Tom, and Beryl had eyes and ears only for the nice-looking lad, no one overheard what passed between them.

"Miss Robin, I would never have forgiven myself if anything had happened to you! You should not have taken such a risk - just for my model."

Robin looked at Dale with shining eyes. Would she tell him of her "pretend?"

"*you* saved *my* life once," she exclaimed, impulsively.

"*I* did!"

"Yes - a long time ago. I was hunting in a little park in New York for my doll that I'd left there and you found me, crying. And you took me home - to Patchin Place. I guess maybe you forgot, because you were big and I was a little bit of a thing!"

Dale stared at her for a moment, then he laughed.

"Why, of *course* - I remember now. You *were* a little bit of a thing, with blue eyes and a blue tam. You asked me what a Ma was! Yes, I'd clean forgotten." He sobered suddenly, and Robin knew it was because he remembered *why* he had forgotten. His father had been hurt that evening.

He looked very big now and very much grown up and Robin wondered, with a wild confusion sending her blood tingling to her face, would he remember that she had kissed him and called him her Prince? She watched him, trembling. But no, he did not remember!

"Well, you've more than repaid me for *that* little thing," he said. "Someone else would have found you if I hadn't. And please promise, Miss Robin, you won't take any more chances for me!"

So Robin locked her precious "pretend" away in her heart - not to be forgotten, but to be enjoyed, as a big-little girl enjoys taking out childish toys or dolls or fancies, dusting them carefully, caressing them tenderly, putting them back reverently - and feeling tremendously grown-up!

*   *   *   *   *

A silvery, shimmery young moon shone down upon two heads close together at a wide-open window. The one was dark and the other red. And the same young moon audaciously winked at the whispered confidences exchanged in the brooding quiet of the night.

"Oh, Robin, doesn't it seem an *age* since you went off to Granger's? - So much has happened. I don't feel like the same girl - Tom Granger's awfully nice looking - his eyes are *blue*, Robin - oh, I won't let myself *think* of going to New York until Mom and Pop are settled somewhere away from the Mills - Robin, you're so *quiet* - I should think you'd be bursting -"

"I'm glad my aunt was nice to Susy and your mother and - Dale. Beryl, she's going to make Norris take that invention -"

"Well, I never dreamed that old toy really amounted to anything -"

" _ _   _ _   _ _ _ "

"Beryl, don't you love the stars? *You're* quiet now -"

Beryl giggled.

"Robin - I just remembered! Do you realize we gave our - Queen - *her own book for Christmas?*"

"Beryl, as *sure* as anything! Oh, how funny!"

EPILOGUE

A STORY AFTER THE STORY

In a hammock hung between two leafing apple trees, a woman lay, so very still that she seemed sleeping. A fitful breeze stirred the pale foliage over her head, now and then showering her with pink petals from the lingering blossoms; from beneath her rose the damp sweet fragrance of soft earth and green grass, nearby a meadow-lark sang plaintively; somewhere a robin called arrogantly to his mate in the nest; from the valley, stretching below the sloping orchard, a violet mist lifted.

A tender smile played over the lips of the reclining woman and her eyes stared through the lacy canopy of green into the blue sky, where fleecy clouds sailed off to the west and south.

A lingering echo went singing through her heart. "It is all yours, Moira Lynch! It is all yours!" The beauty around her - the promise of spring, the green of orchard and meadow and distant hill, the rest, the contentment - the happiness, and oh, most precious, the fulfilment.

There was never a day now, in Mother Moira's life, so busy that she could not snatch a moment to go over, in reverent appreciation, the blessings that were hers. And no longer were her dreams - for nothing could change the dreaming heart of the little woman - for herself or even for her big Danny; they were for her fine lad, a man now, and Beryl, working so earnestly for her ambition, and little Robin, who would always *be* little Robin, and the imp of a Susy, ruddy cheeked and happy-hearted.

How long, long ago seemed those days when, a slip of a girl, she had dreamed on that other hillside of a future that would be hers; how dazzling had been the pictures she had fancied; how much she had dared to ask. In her youthful bravado she had laughed at Destiny and had made so bold as to declare Destiny might even then be weaving a bit of gold into the drab fabric of her life.

(Faith, was not little Robin her bit of gold? Had not the wonderful change begun in their lives after little Robin came to the Manor?)

Five years had passed, since she and her big Danny had moved from the village to the little farm that was "just around the corner." During them she and big Danny had been alone a great deal of the time, excepting for little Susy; for Dale and Beryl, after settling them snugly in the old-fashioned farmhouse, (painted as white as white with a new barn for the gentle-eyed cow, and a pen for the pigs, and a trim little run-way for the chickens) had gone away, Dale to an engineering college, Beryl to live with Miss Allendyce and take her precious violin lessons, and lessons in languages and science. But Mother Moira was never lonesome, for mere miles could not separate a heart like hers from those she loved!

There had been significant changes in the village for her to watch develop. The old Mill cottages had been torn down and across the river had been built a cluster of white houses, each with its own yard "going right around it," and trees and a bit of garden. There was a new school house, too, and a new corps of teachers, and a hospital and a library. Robin and her aunt had opened this only a month before.

And the House of Laughter had been enlarged to meet the increasing demands upon it; there were rooms for the girls' clubs and the boys' clubs, and a billiard room and a bowling alley, and an athletic field with a basketball court and a baseball diamond.

(Sir Galahad in his scarlet coat still hung over the mantel which Williams had built. Robin would not let anyone change that.)

Mrs. Riley lived in the upper floor of the House of Laughter and took care of it.

The Manor car, with Madame Forsyth, passed often now through the streets of the village and from it Madame nodded pleasantly to this person and that, stopping sometimes to ask one Mill mother concerning her sick child, another of her husband - and another whether she had finished the knit bed-spread upon which Madame had found her working one afternoon when she had called. Madame had herself regularly visited the new Mill houses during the process of construction and took delight in dropping in upon the newly organized school while classes were in session.

"I'll be the same proud, overbearing old lady," she had told her lawyer, but she had been mistaken - she could never be quite that again, for she had found too much pure delight in doing the little things Robin quite artlessly suggested - little things which had not been easy at first and which had seemed to demand too great a sacrifice of her pride.

The passing of time for the three at the Manor, Madame, Mrs. Budge and Harkness, was marked, Mother Lynch well knew, by Robin's coming and going. For, when her Jimmie had returned from southern seas, Robin had insisted upon going straight to him, and it was not until her aunt had laid aside the last shred of her old prejudice and invited Robin's father to the Manor for a long visit that Robin had consented to look upon the Manor as her "home," though, even then, she steadfastly asserted "part" of her time must be spent with Jimmie.

While at the Manor James Forsyth had painted his "Wood

Sprite," which won for him quick and wide recognition, and ever afterward Robin and Madame Forsyth referred to it as "our picture."

No, Mother Moira was never lonesome.

A gay voice roused her now from her happy reverie, footsteps rustled the grass, cool hands, with a touch as light as the blowing petals, closed over her eyes.

"Dreaming again, little Mom? You're incurable!" And Beryl, with a laugh, dropped upon the ground close to the hammock, one hand closing over her mother's.

"It's a bit of a cat-nap I'm stealing," fibbed Mother Moira, blushing like a girl. Her eyes lingered adoringly on the glowing, flushed face close to hers. "Where have you been, Beryl?"

"Susy coaxed me off to her fairy spring. It's really a lovely little nook she's found and she's made a doll's house in the hollow of an old tree. She's a funny little thing - almost elfin, isn't she? Are you sure she isn't too much trouble for you and Dad, Mother?"

"Trouble? Bless the little heart of the colleen, it's something happening every minute for it's an imp of mischief she is, but, Beryl, I like it. It keeps my own heart young."

"As though your heart would ever grow old! You're like Robin. Oh, mother, you can't *know* how lonesome I've been over there in Milan for the sight of you and this little place. I think my soul, the one poor dear Jacques Henri tried to find in me and didn't - wakened one night when I actually cried myself to sleep just longing to feel your arms around me! Oh, when one has a mother and a home like mine to want to come to, it ought to be *easy* to keep beautiful inside, the way the dear man said!" And Beryl, staring thoughtfully out over the valley, did not see the glow that transformed her mother's face.

Jane Abbott

A shrill whistle from the Mills echoed and reechoed through the valley. Beryl turned her head suddenly and laid her cheek against the palm of her mother's hand.

"Mother, I saw a lot of Tom Granger when I was in Paris."

Mother Moira started ever so slightly, with the barest twitching of the hand Beryl's cheek touched.

"He was very nice to me. Mother, are he and - and Robin - awfully good friends?"

"What's in your heart, my girl?"

"Mom, couldn't Robin marry almost *anybody*? She's such a dear and she's so rich and she's travelled around so much."

"Why, bless the heart of her, she's nothing but a child!"

"Mother!" Beryl's voice rang impatiently. "We'll just *never* grow up in your eyes! Why, Robin's twenty. Well, I should think *anyone'd* like Tom Granger."

"Oh, my dear!" And Mother Moira, reading the girl's heart with her wise mother-eyes, gave a tiny sigh. Must the shadow of a heartache touch the splendid friendship between these two, Beryl and Robin?

The thought lingered with her while she watched the girls come hand in hand out to the orchard from the drive where Robin had left her roadster. Beryl had only been home for three days and Robin came out to the farm at every opportunity.

Her girls - her tall, handsome Beryl with the strong shoulders and the free swing of her, and little Robin, with her deep blue eyes and her tender lips and her alive hair, and the little limp that gave her walk the appearance of eagerness.

There was still so much to talk about that the two girls lingered under the trees while Mother Moira swung gently and listened and watched the dear young faces. Beryl had been the guest for a weekend at a duke's house; Robin had spent a month in the Canadian Rockies with her Jimmie; Dale had brought home all sorts of tales of adventures from an expedition he had made with an engineering gang into the fastnesses of South America, and Beryl had been asked to tour in the fall with the Cincinnati Symphony and was going to accept. Their chatter came back then to Wassumsic and the new hospital and the library and the new teachers, who were Smith College graduates, and Sophie Mack who had started a Girl Scout troop, and the new athletic field at the House of Laughter.

"Bless me, it's forgetting the supper I am, and Dale coming!" cried Mother Moira, springing to quick life.

"And Dale has a wonderful secret to tell, too," laughed Robin, her eyes shining.

Beryl looked at her friend curiously - Robin had the "all-tight-inside" look that Beryl remembered from the old days at the Manor.

"Do you know the secret?" she asked.

Robin's face flushed rose-red. "Y-yes. But I promised Dale I wouldn't tell. We both want to see your mother's face - when she hears it."

"Well, I think you're mean to have a secret with Dale that *I* don't know!" cried Beryl, with real indignation. "Is it something that's going to make Mom lots happier?"

"I - hope - so!" And to hide the tell-tale rose on her face Robin threw her arms around Mother Moira and kissed her.

"Faith, is it any happier I could be without my heart

just breaking?"

Dale came and they all, big Danny in his wheel chair, ate supper on the broad porch where they could enjoy the sunset. Beryl watched her brother with admiring eyes - he had grown so strong and big and good-looking, his nice-fitting clothes set off his broad shoulders so well, his voice had such a ring of confidence.

"I've been offered the management of the Forsyth Mills," he announced suddenly.

Then *that* was the secret!

"Really, truly?" exclaimed Beryl.

"And will ye take it, my boy?" asked big Danny, a note of pride deepening his voice.

"My boy a manager!" trilled Mother Moira.

"Yes. I'll take it. I made one condition with Madame Forsyth - and she granted it." And Dale flashed a look across to Robin. Everyone followed his glance and everyone read the truth in Robin's face.

"Robin Forsyth - and you never breathed a *word*!" cried Beryl, not knowing for the moment whether to give way to great joy or indignation that her friend had not confided in her.

With a quick little motion, Robin had slipped to Mother Lynch's chair and, kneeling beside it, she buried her face against the woman's heart.

"I didn't know - myself," came in muffled tones from the embrace.

"Are you happy, mother?" asked Dale, boyishly.

"Ah, I did not know I could be happier - but, I am!" And Mother Moira smiled through the tears that brimmed in her eyes.

Beryl, staring at her mother and brother and her friend, suddenly gave voice to a thought that had come with such significance as to sweep away her girlish reserve.

"Then it *isn't* Tom Granger at all! You don't care a *bit* about him?"

Robin's face lifted. "About Tom? Oh, goodness me, no. Why, he isn't worth Dale's little *finger* - Beryl Lynch, why do you ask me that?"

"Oh - nothing. Really, truly -" And Beryl escaped into the house.

*   *   *   *   *

Robin drove Dale back to the village. At the turn of the road near theHouse of Laughter she stopped the car that they might enjoy for a moment the twilight glow of the valley. Lights twinkled from the Mill houses across the river. From the House of Laughter came the sound of singing. A young crescent of a moon shone silvery against a purple blue sky.

"Little Red-Robin," cried Dale, suddenly, "Are you very sure?"

"Sure - of what?" Robin asked in a voice that trembled in spite of her.

"Someday you will be a rich girl. I am a - working-man. What will the world say? They may laugh at you!"

Robin's chin lifted. Had she ever reckoned her gifts in dollars and cents?

"But you're my Prince!" she protested, proudly. "Don't you

remember? That night, a long, long time ago, when you took me home, I called you - my Prince. You said, then, you couldn't stay with me - that I'd have to find you. Well," her voice dropped to a whisper, "I have."

Choose from Thousands of 1stWorldLibrary Classics By

A. M. Barnard
Ada Leverson
Adolphus William Ward
Aesop
Agatha Christie
Alexander Aaronsohn
Alexander Kielland
Alexandre Dumas
Alfred Gatty
Alfred Ollivant
Alice Duer Miller
Alice Turner Curtis
Alice Dunbar
Allen Chapman
Ambrose Bierce
Amelia E. Barr
Amory H. Bradford
Andrew Lang
Andrew McFarland Davis
Andy Adams
Anna Alice Chapin
Anna Sewell
Annie Besant
Annie Hamilton Donnell
Annie Payson Call
Annie Roe Carr
Annonaymous
Anton Chekhov
Arnold Bennett
Arthur Conan Doyle
Arthur M. Winfield
Arthur Ransome
Arthur Schnitzler
Atticus
B.H. Baden-Powell
B. M. Bower
B. C. Chatterjee
Baroness Emmuska Orczy
Baroness Orczy
Basil King
Bayard Taylor
Ben Macomber
Bertha Muzzy Bower
Bjornstjerne Bjornson
Booth Tarkington
Boyd Cable
Bram Stoker
C. Collodi
C. E. Orr

C. M. Ingleby
Carolyn Wells
Catherine Parr Traill
Charles A. Eastman
Charles Amory Beach
Charles Dickens
Charles Dudley Warner
Charles Farrar Browne
Charles Ives
Charles Kingsley
Charles Klein
Charles Hanson Towne
Charles Lathrop Pack
Charles Romyn Dake
Charles Whibley
Charles Willing Beale
Charlotte M. Braeme
Charlotte M. Yonge
Charlotte Perkins Stetson
Clair W. Hayes
Clarence Day Jr.
Clarence E. Mulford
Clemence Housman
Confucius
Coningsby Dawson
Cornelis DeWitt Wilcox
Cyril Burleigh
D. H. Lawrence
Daniel Defoe
David Garnett
Dinah Craik
Don Carlos Janes
Donald Keyhoe
Dorothy Kilner
Dougan Clark
Douglas Fairbanks
E. Nesbit
E.P.Roe
E. Phillips Oppenheim
Earl Barnes
Edgar Rice Burroughs
Edith Van Dyne
Edith Wharton
Edward Everett Hale
Edward J. O'Biren
Edward S. Ellis
Edwin L. Arnold
Eleanor Atkins
Eliot Gregory

Elizabeth Gaskell
Elizabeth McCracken
Elizabeth Von Arnim
Ellem Key
Emerson Hough
Emilie F. Carlen
Emily Dickinson
Enid Bagnold
Enilor Macartney Lane
Erasmus W. Jones
Ernie Howard Pie
Ethel May Dell
Ethel Turner
Ethel Watts Mumford
Eugenie Foa
Eugene Wood
Eustace Hale Ball
Evelyn Everett-green
Everard Cotes
F. H. Cheley
F. J. Cross
F. Marion Crawford
Federick Austin Ogg
Ferdinand Ossendowski
Francis Bacon
Francis Darwin
Frances Hodgson Burnett
Frances Parkinson Keyes
Frank Gee Patchin
Frank Harris
Frank Jewett Mather
Frank L. Packard
Frank V. Webster
Frederic Stewart Isham
Frederick Trevor Hill
Frederick Winslow Taylor
Friedrich Kerst
Friedrich Nietzsche
Fyodor Dostoyevsky
G.A. Henty
G.K. Chesterton
Gabrielle E. Jackson
Garrett P. Serviss
Gaston Leroux
George A. Warren
George Ade
Geroge Bernard Shaw
George Durston
George Ebers

George Eliot
George Gissing
George MacDonald
George Meredith
George Orwell
George Sylvester Viereck
George Tucker
George W. Cable
George Wharton James
Gertrude Atherton
Gordon Casserly
Grace E. King
Grace Gallatin
Grace Greenwood
Grant Allen
Guillermo A. Sherwell
Gulielma Zollinger
Gustav Flaubert
H. A. Cody
H. B. Irving
H.C. Bailey
H. G. Wells
H. H. Munro
H. Irving Hancock
H. Rider Haggard
H. W. C. Davis
Haldeman Julius
Hall Caine
Hamilton Wright Mabie
Hans Christian Andersen
Harold Avery
Harold McGrath
Harriet Beecher Stowe
Harry Castlemon
Harry Coghill
Harry Houidini
Hayden Carruth
Helent Hunt Jackson
Helen Nicolay
Hendrik Conscience
Hendy David Thoreau
Henri Barbusse
Henrik Ibsen
Henry Adams
Henry Ford
Henry Frost
Henry James
Henry Jones Ford
Henry Seton Merriman
Henry W Longfellow
Herbert A. Giles

Herbert Carter
Herbert N. Casson
Herman Hesse
Hildegard G. Frey
Homer
Honore De Balzac
Horace B. Day
Horace Walpole
Horatio Alger Jr.
Howard Pyle
Howard R. Garis
Hugh Lofting
Hugh Walpole
Humphry Ward
Ian Maclaren
Inez Haynes Gillmore
Irving Bacheller
Isabel Hornibrook
Israel Abrahams
Ivan Turgenev
J.G.Austin
J. Henri Fabre
J. M. Barrie
J. Macdonald Oxley
J. S. Fletcher
J. S. Knowles
J. Storer Clouston
Jack London
Jacob Abbott
James Allen
James Andrews
James Baldwin
James Branch Cabell
James DeMille
James Joyce
James Lane Allen
James Lane Allen
James Oliver Curwood
James Oppenheim
James Otis
James R. Driscoll
Jane Austen
Jane L. Stewart
Janet Aldridge
Jens Peter Jacobsen
Jerome K. Jerome
John Burroughs
John Cournos
John F. Kennedy
John Gay
John Glasworthy

John Habberton
John Joy Bell
John Kendrick Bangs
John Milton
John Philip Sousa
Jonas Lauritz Idemil Lie
Jonathan Swift
Joseph A. Altsheler
Joseph Carey
Joseph Conrad
Joseph E. Badger Jr
Joseph Hergesheimer
Joseph Jacobs
Jules Vernes
Julian Hawthrone
Julie A Lippmann
Justin Huntly McCarthy
Kakuzo Okakura
Kenneth Grahame
Kenneth McGaffey
Kate Langley Bosher
Kate Langley Bosher
Katherine Cecil Thurston
Katherine Stokes
L. A. Abbot
L. T. Meade
L. Frank Baum
Latta Griswold
Laura Dent Crane
Laura Lee Hope
Laurence Housman
Lawrence Beasley
Leo Tolstoy
Leonid Andreyev
Lewis Carroll
Lewis Sperry Chafer
Lilian Bell
Lloyd Osbourne
Louis Hughes
Louis Tracy
Louisa May Alcott
Lucy Fitch Perkins
Lucy Maud Montgomery
Luther Benson
Lydia Miller Middleton
Lyndon Orr
M. Corvus
M. H. Adams
Margaret E. Sangster
Margret Howth
Margaret Vandercook

Margret Penrose
Maria Edgeworth
Maria Thompson Daviess
Mariano Azuela
Marion Polk Angellotti
Mark Overton
Mark Twain
Mary Austin
Mary Catherine Crowley
Mary Cole
Mary Hastings Bradley
Mary Roberts Rinehart
Mary Rowlandson
M. Wollstonecraft Shelley
Maud Lindsay
Max Beerbohm
Myra Kelly
Nathaniel Hawthrone
Nicolo Machiavelli
O. F. Walton
Oscar Wilde
Owen Johnson
P.G. Wodehouse
Paul and Mabel Thorne
Paul G. Tomlinson
Paul Severing
Percy Brebner
Peter B. Kyne
Plato
R. Derby Holmes
R. L. Stevenson
R. S. Ball
Rabindranath Tagore
Rahul Alvares
Ralph Bonehill
Ralph Henry Barbour
Ralph Victor
Ralph Waldo Emmerson
Rene Descartes
Rex Beach

Rex E. Beach
Richard Harding Davis
Richard Jefferies
Richard Le Gallienne
Robert Barr
Robert Frost
Robert Gordon Anderson
Robert L. Drake
Robert Lansing
Robert Lynd
Robert Michael Ballantyne
Robert W. Chambers
Rosa Nouchette Carey
Rudyard Kipling
Samuel B. Allison
Samuel Hopkins Adams
Sarah Bernhardt
Sarah C. Hallowell
Selma Lagerlof
Sherwood Anderson
Sigmund Freud
Standish O'Grady
Stanley Weyman
Stella Benson
Stella M. Francis
Stephen Crane
Stewart Edward White
Stijn Streuvels
Swami Abhedananda
Swami Parmananda
T. S. Ackland
T. S. Arthur
The Princess Der Ling
Thomas A. Janvier
Thomas A Kempis
Thomas Anderton
Thomas Bailey Aldrich
Thomas Bulfinch
Thomas De Quincey
Thomas Dixon

Thomas H. Huxley
Thomas Hardy
Thomas More
Thornton W. Burgess
U. S. Grant
Valentine Williams
Various Authors
Vaughan Kester
Victor Appleton
Victoria Cross
Virginia Woolf
Wadsworth Camp
Walter Camp
Walter Scott
Washington Irving
Wilbur Lawton
Wilkie Collins
Willa Cather
Willard F. Baker
William Dean Howells
William le Queux
W. Makepeace Thackeray
William W. Walter
William Shakespeare
Winston Churchill
Yei Theodora Ozaki
Yogi Ramacharaka
Young E. Allison
Zane Grey

www.ingramcontent.com/pod-product-compliance
Lightning Source LLC
Chambersburg PA
CBHW030754150426
42813CB00068B/3047/J